The Healthy Vegetarian

The Healthy Vegetarian

by Sri Swami Satchidananda

with a Foreword by Dean Ornish, M.D.
and a special section on getting started
by Sandra McLanahan, M.D.
and Swami Premananda Ma

Integral Yoga® Publications
Yogaville, Virginia

Library of Congress Cataloging-in-Publication Data
Satchidananda, Swami
    The healthy vegetarian.

    Bibliography: p.

    1. Vegetarianism.   I. Title.
TX392.S28   1986   613.2'62   86-2974
ISBN 0-932040-32-2

Integral Yoga® Publications
Route 1, Box 172
Buckingham, Virginia 23921, U.S.A.

Printed in the United States of America.

Foreword

Science is beginning to prove the health benefits of a low-fat, vegetarian diet. Coronary heart disease is still the number one cause of death and disability in this country, and it has been strongly linked with cholesterol intake.

Vegetarians have much lower rates of coronary disease than those eating the typical American diet. This is not so surprising when one considers that cholesterol is found only in animal products. Many studies have shown that elevated blood levels of cholesterol are strongly correlated with risk of coronary heart disease, and that one's blood level of cholesterol is directly related to the amount of dietary cholesterol. Animal products also tend to be high in saturated fat, which the body converts into cholesterol.

High blood pressure is another risk factor for coronary heart disease and stroke. People who eat a vegetarian diet tend to have not only lower blood levels of cholesterol but also lower blood pressure than those eating a non-vegetarian diet. For example, in a research study published recently in the *Journal of the American Medical Association,* my colleagues and I found that vegetarians living in the Satchidananda Ashram had lower serum cholesterol and lower blood pressure than a comparable group of people living in Framingham, Massachusetts. Other studies have shown that feeding meat to vegetarians causes their blood pressure to rise independent of other factors such as emotional stress.

We have also conducted research demonstrating that a vegetarian diet can help treat as well as help prevent coronary heart disease. Even patients who had severe coronary heart disease demonstrated rather remarkable subjective and objective improvements in just a few weeks after following a vegetarian diet and practicing yoga techniques on a daily basis.

The benefits of a vegetarian diet are not limited to heart disease. Recent evidence suggests that the most common forms of cancer are also influenced by diet. Cancers of the breast, colon, prostate and lung are significantly lower in those who eat a vegetarian diet and who do not smoke. Dietary factors are no doubt important in other illnesses as well.

While researchers have not yet proven some of the benefits that Sri Swamiji describes in this book, it may be just a matter of time before they do. In the meantime, there is already enough evidence for us to move toward the vegetarian end of the food spectrum. As a physician, a well-balanced vegetarian diet—rather than "mono-diet" or "living on air"—makes the most sense to me.

I remain indebted to Sri Swami Satchidananda for first teaching me the benefits of a vegetarian diet. Ultimately, he teaches that health and longevity are not ends in themselves—after all, we are all going to die eventually. But health is the first step toward leading a useful and joyful life.

With best wishes,

Sincerely,

Dean Ornish, M.D.
Clinical Instructor of Medicine
University of California, San Francisco

Preface

The author of this book, Sri Swami Satchidananda, is a modern day Yoga Master. As a native of India, Yoga's original home, Sri Swamiji grew up steeped in Yogic tradition. Having achieved the experience of "the peace that passeth all understanding," he travels the world over, invited by groups and institutions, sharing the teachings of Yoga, including some of its ramifications in the fields of health, world peace, and religious unity.

People often ask him, "Do you have a prescription for a healthy diet?" His gentle and non-dogmatic answer is, "I would never want to give a 'prescription' for a healthy diet, because one person's nectar is another's poison. Constitutions vary, life styles vary, so each one has to decide what is best for him or her. But I would generally recommend any diet that would not deposit toxins into the system, that would be easily digested and would give enough nutrition."

But, seeing how active and healthy the septuagenarian Swami is—and knowing him to be a lifelong vegetarian—the questioning often turns to his personal choice, that of vegetarianism. He has this to say about his own experience of diet:

"I have been a vegetarian all of my life. I work day and night. I travel twenty days out of the month. Today I am in Virginia, tomorrow I might be in Dallas, Texas, the next day in London. Almost every day I am lecturing and meeting people, and with all that I eat only once a day and only vegetarian food. And when I am not traveling, I do manual work also. I drive a tractor, operate heavy equipment, ride a horse. My perspiration is always clean, sometimes sweet-smelling, like sandalwood. In fact, I have tried going for an entire month without taking a bath and I never smell-ed bad. I don't fall sick; I never even get the "common cold" or headache. At one time a doctor wanted to test the health of my internal organs. He found that my kidneys and heart were those of a twenty-five year old. My chiropractor says I have the spine of an eighteen year old. I sleep very little, only a few hours a night."

This testimonial may inspire us, and yet leave us with many questions about vegetarianism and diet. The first section of this book shares Sri Swamiji's thoughts on many aspects of vegetarianism, from issues of physical health and questions of morality to a discussion of the effects of meat diet and vegetarian diet upon our minds. He also tackles psychological and moral issues such as dealing with non-vegetarian family members and even dealing with insect pests on home-grown vegetables. The second section is a compendium of his advice on specific issues pertaining to Yogic diet.

Chandrika Vonne
Editor

Acknowledgements

I would like to thank Chandrika Vonne for her fine efforts in gathering this material and preparing the manuscript for publication. Also, Dr. Dean Ornish for writing the Foreword to this book and Dr. Sandra McLanahan and Swami Premananda Ma for contributing the section on helping beginning vegetarians get started.

My sincere appreciation to Swami Sharadananda Ma, Swami Prakashananda Ma and Abhaya Thiele of Integral Yoga Publications and to Prema Serre and Gretchen Uma Knight, the Production Coordinators for this project.

Table of Contents

PART II — THE BASICS OF YOGIC DIET

PART III — GETTING STARTED

Part I:

Why Should I Be a Vegetarian?

Two healthy vegetarians.

Introduction to Vegetarian Life

"Why should someone want to become a vegetarian?" Many, many people have asked me this question. And in this scientific age most people want to see some proof of the benefit of something before they try it. So I would like to share with you the results of one study with which I was involved.

In 1977, I was invited to speak at the Baylor College of Medicine in Houston, Texas. More coronary bypass operations are performed in the medical center there than anywhere else in the United States. The students and doctors were very interested in my talk about vegetarian diet and Yoga.

One of the medical doctors at Baylor, a student of mine named Dean Ornish, wanted to study the effect of vegetarian diet and Yoga on coronary heart disease. He worked with a group of patients who had acute problems, many of which could not be corrected by surgery. The Plaza Hotel in Houston generously donated one month's use of ten rooms for the study. Some of the patients spent the entire time there; others went to work during the day and came "home" to the hotel at night. All of them were put on a program of strict vegetarian diet, simple Yoga postures and breathing exercises, progressive deep relaxation and healing visualization.

After one month, most of the patients demonstrated substantial improvement. Many became pain free. Many of those who wanted to go back to work full-time were able to do so. Most important, tests indicated that the heart was able to receive an increased blood flow through such treatment. This had never been documented in such a way before.[1]

Later, we repeated the study in a more definitive way. In this second study, forty-eight heart patient volunteers were randomly divided into two equal groups. One group had the program of vegetarian diet and Yoga for three and a half weeks; the other group received only their usual medical care during the same period. When tested after the program, the vegetarian group showed substantial improvements. These patients experienced a 91% reduction of angina (chest pain), increased exercise capability, reduced blood pressure and reduced cholesterol levels. Nuclear cardiology tests indicated that each one's heart was beating and pumping blood more effectively. In contrast, the control group showed none of these improvements.[2]

Other scientific studies have also been conducted on vegetarianism and have also showed very positive effects.[3] Why is this? There are many reasons, some of which I will present on the following pages. We should know, however, that health considerations are not the only arguments in favor of a vegetarian diet. We can look, too, from the points of view of philosophy, religion, ethics, ecology and economics. We can consider what kind of foods our bodies are physiologically designed for. And for those interested in the effects of food on our minds, we can look at what kind of diet is most conducive to our mental well-being. Considering even one of these points is likely to make us think more seriously about adopting a vegetarian diet. When we look at all of them, the evidence becomes quite convincing. So, for the sake of our physical and mental well-being, and for the well-being of our beloved planet Earth, I present the following facts about vegetarianism. It is my sincere hope and prayer that this information might help open your mind to new possibilities for a healthier, happier life.

Our Natural Diet

Let us first consider the question, "What is the natural diet for human beings?" When we look at the diet of mammals, we find two major groups: the flesh-eating animals, such as dogs, cats, tigers and lions; and the vegetarian animals, such as cows, bulls, horses, camels, monkeys - and even the largest land animal, the elephant. Comparing their physical features, the flesh-eating animals have long teeth to tear the raw animal flesh from the bones, while the vegetarian animals all have flat teeth for grinding vegetable food. Meat-eating animals have rough tongues to lick the flesh from the bone and sharp, strong claws to catch and kill their prey, while vegetarian animals do not. The meat-eaters also have excellent night vision for hunting, while the vegetarians have more difficulty seeing after dusk.

These are just the external features that can be seen. There are others, which we cannot see. The intestines of meat-eating animals are only about two to three times their body length. That means that the meat they eat can pass through their systems quickly before it putrifies. Vegetarian animals' intestines are about six or seven times their bodies' length, because their systems need not push the food through so rapidly. The vegetarians have a different pH in their saliva and their stomachs than the meat-eaters; vegetarians also have digestive enzymes in their saliva, and begin digesting while the food is still in the mouth, while meat-eaters gulp their food without much chewing.

Now let us look at the human animal. Human beings have flat, grinding teeth - like the vegetarians. They do not have the rough tongues or sharp claws of the meat-eaters. Humans also have more difficulty seeing after dusk. Their intestines are about 26 feet long - or six to seven times their body's length - like the vegetarians. The pH of their saliva is similar to vegetarians', and it contains digestive enzymes. So the evidence seems indisputable: by physical design, we are certainly vegetarian animals.

You might argue, "What about the Eskimos whose diet is primarily meat? How can you tell them that they are vegetarians by nature and should give up meat? They would starve!" I would never advocate vegetarian diet in such an environment where even grass does not grow. If vegetable food will not grow, certainly we must eat animals. Why stop there? If nothing else is available, people will even eat each other. We have seen this happen at various times in the world. It may be difficult for us to admit, but it is a fact. We have to survive. But when we *can* get the food most suited to our natures, certainly we should do so. If you still want to use the Eskimos as an example, you should note that the average life span of an Eskimo is twenty-seven and a half years! Compare this with the life span of the Hunzas of Pakistan, whose diet is primarily vegetarian. Recorded ages of 110 are not uncommon among their population.

Food: Its Effects on Body and Mind

If you want to see the differences between flesh-eating and vegetarian animals very clearly, go to the zoo. Look carefully at the different animals. The meat-eating animals all need to be caged: the tigers, the lions, the leopards. Even inside their cages, they are restless, pacing endlessly back and forth. They are fierce and aggressive. And you may even hesitate to go near their cages because they smell so bad. Everything that comes out of their bodies smells foul. The vegetarian animals, on the other hand, are calm and gentle; they are not frightening. Often they do not even need to be caged; they walk slowly, peacefully. They can be allowed to roam around freely. And their bodies do not smell bad. You can even put your nose right into the mouth of a cow and not find any foul smell. It is the same with their perspiration, their urine, their excrement. If you have been to India, you might know that cow dung is used to clean the floors there. Pick up a piece of cow dung and smell it; there is no bad smell at all. Can you comfortably smell the dung of a dog?

Why should flesh-eating animals smell bad while vegetarian ones do not? It is because of the food they eat. That is why almost all meat-eating people cannot expose their armpits without embarrassment! They have to constantly spray deodorants to cover up the foul smell, because what they eat comes out through their pores. If you are a strict vegetarian with a clean diet, your perspiration will not smell bad. Many meat-eating people will never take off their

6

shoes in the presence of others because their feet smell so bad. If you are a vegetarian you need not worry about such things. Even if you do not take a bath for ten days, your body will not smell bad.

So, in both physical and mental conditions, carnivores differ from herbivores. As you know, mostly all soldiers in wartime eat a diet high in meat. If you give them Yogic food - milk and fruit for example - they will not fight. We feed them meat, expecting them to act like wild animals. However, some of the commanders who direct them are vegetarians because they have to think clearly. When I am asked, "Is there any way of stopping war?", I often answer, "Send the soldiers barrels of milk and honey, fruits and nuts; stop the war 'drum and rum', play some symphonic music." The meat, the war drum and the liquor all affect the minds of the soldiers. It makes them *rajasic* - restless, warlike. Without all that they would just throw away their guns and sit and meditate. That is the power of food and of sound vibration.

Health Considerations

LIVE VS. DEAD FOOD

We have looked at the effects of vegetarian diet on the mind and at some of its physical effects. But there is much more that can be said about the relationship between vegetarian diet and health. The vegetarian diet is the best diet known for promoting good health. A diet of fruit, vegetables, grains, legumes, nuts and milk products will not leave a lot of toxins in our systems. It is the animal matter that leaves so much toxic material. Why? Because the minute you kill an animal, its body, its corpse, starts to decay. Once the animal is killed, it is dead matter. We are literally eating dead matter. This is not the case with vegetables. They may dehydrate, but it will be a very long time before they decay. Eat half of a vegetable and plant the other half. It will grow again. It is still a living organism. Take the stem of a spinach plant, cut it into ten parts. Eat the leaves, but plant the pieces of stem and you will get ten new spinach plants. Can you do that with a lamb? Can you eat its leg and then make the other parts grow into another lamb? No, because it is dead matter.

TOXICITY OF MEAT

People sometimes think it is possible to find healthy animals to eat. But even if the veterinarian has certified that an animal is healthy before slaughter, at the time of killing what happens to its system? What happens to *your* system when you are frightened? Adrenalin courses throughout the body, affecting every cell. The same thing happens within an animal. At the moment of slaughter, all kinds of undesirable toxins and hormones get splashed into the body. Where do they go after that? Nowhere; they remain in the meat that comes to your table.

Because our intestines are so long, approximately twenty-two to twenty-six feet, the decayed flesh cannot be digested and pass through before it putrifies. Although the body tries to filter out the toxins through the eliminative system (the perspiration, the breath, etc.), *all* of the toxins are not eliminated. It is these wastes remaining in the system that thicken the arteries with cholesterol, often causing atherosclerosis, and eventually high blood pressure, strokes and heart attacks.[4]

It is the elimination of these toxins that causes foul perspiration odor. If everyone were to become a vegetarian, we could close all the deodorant factories. We often see television commercials in which a young man (or woman) comes up to talk to a young woman (or man), only to have her make a face and run away. So he goes and sprays something in his mouth and then all the girls come flocking around him! How long can people live on a spray? If they really want to attract others, let them live on pure vegetarian food. The perspiration of a person who lives on pure food will have a scent like flowers; it might even be sweet, like jasmine or sandalwood.

When such a person moves his or her bowels, there will be no need to wash or use toilet paper. Don't we see this even in a goat? The excrement comes out very smoothly in small black balls covered with a kind of white coating; it does not even soil the goat's body. We can have that kind of elimination. When you eat the proper food in the proper quantity, your excreta is formulated well; it passes through in softish balls and never smells bad. If it smells or is clay-like or too loose, something is wrong in the stomach or intestines.

PROTEIN

Many people are concerned about getting enough protein. It is true that there is a lot of protein in meat, but we do not need that concentrated a protein in our systems. It is not a simple form of protein, but one that is very concentrated, very rich. Even the meat-eating animals try to eat only *vegetarian* animals. Meat-eating humans also eat only vegetarian animals. They would never eat a carnivorous animal. Our protein should be as close to its natural source as possible. A vegetarian animal gives us better protein than a meat-eating one; eating the vegetables themselves is better still. There is plenty of protein in beans like soy and lentils, in avocados, nuts, seeds and dairy products. There it is found in a simple form that is easy to digest and assimilate.

FLEXIBILITY AND EASE

Vegetarians have bodies that are healthier and more supple than the bodies of meat-eaters. They also have much less tension in their bodies. The moment a person changes from a meat diet, he or she will feel a lightness and a release of tension. I have heard this over and over again. Yoga postures and other forms of exercise become easier, and sometimes long-standing complaints - such as insomnia or nervousness - disappear.

PHYSICAL STRENGTH

Some people are concerned about how they will be able to keep up their strength without having meat in their diet. I would recommend that they ask Mr. Elephant. The elephants are the biggest and strongest animals in the world, and they are pure vegetarians. Some clever minds will argue, "But a tiger can kill an elephant." That is true. Both tigers and elephants are strong. But what kind of strength does the tiger have? Killing strength. What kind of strength does the elephant have? Pulling strength. It can pull ten huge logs at your command. It listens to you, works for you. Can you tie a log to the tail of a tiger and get it to pull it? No. So what kind of strength is more useful to us: restless, killing strength or steady, pulling strength?

Ahimsa: Non-Violence

Many people are concerned about the violence in our society and about the threat which that violence poses to the very existence of our planet. Our meat diet is a part of that violence. We should think about such things, and about adopting a policy of *ahimsa.*

Ahimsa is a Sanskrit word which means non-violence. Following *ahimsa* does not simply mean not killing. We cannot live without destroying other lives. When you eat vegetables, you are killing, destroying something. Even if you do not eat anything, you kill. Do you know how many bacteria you kill each time you take a drink of water? Millions. If it is a matter of avoiding *killing* alone, I would advocate eating meat. Why? Simple mathematical calculations: if you want to eat spinach, how many plants must you kill? Certainly ten or twenty for even one meal. But how many people can eat from just one sheep? Say ten people. If every life you take is one "sin", which is better? Certainly, killing one sheep would be better. So it is not killing we are talking about here. We are talking about non-violence.

What do we mean by violence? If I do something to you and you feel hurt, my act was violent. Causing pain is violence. If we want to be non-violent, our food should come with as little pain as possible. Many people would say, "But plants are alive, too. They feel pain if we pluck and eat them. So why give up meat if not causing pain is the idea?"

Yes, plants have life; animals have life; human beings have life; even an atom has life. In having life we are all equal. But in the expression of consciousness the plant is not as developed as the animal, nor the animal as developed as the human being. Human beings are bestowed with discrimination; it is the human being who even *thinks* of all this, who thinks of comparing himself with other beings. Animals do not compare themselves with humans. Plants are even less developed in the expression of their consciousness. The more developed the expression of consciousness in a particular form of life, the more pain is felt when you destroy it. Cutting off the branch of a tree causes less pain than cutting off the limb of an animal. Many studies show that plants *do* experience pain; but still, we believe it is not as much as the animals experience.

Here is an analogy that might help illustrate this principle. Imagine a classroom of thirty students with a teacher standing in the front of the room, writing on the blackboard. Somewhere in one of the rows two of the students are talking loudly. One is the brightest student in the class. Normally he would not be doing such a thing, but today somehow the other fellow drew him into it. The other boy is "number one" at the other end. He is the worst student, and has no interest in studying at all. He simply came to the classroom because it was even worse at home. So they are both talking. The teacher looks at them and yells, "Hey, you fools, what are you doing there?"

Which of the two do you think would feel most hurt by being called a fool in front of the whole class? The "number one" brilliant boy. The other one might just shrug it off, thinking "I've heard it many times..." Or he might even feel proud: "Finally, the teacher noticed me, paid some attention to me!" But the first one would say, "I'm sorry, I won't do it again!" He might even burst into tears because he has never been addressed like that before. How can the same word create two different feelings in two individuals? One had a sharper, more evolved mind. The other one had a duller mind. It all depends on the development of the consciousness. The bright boy's consciousness was more developed. The other's was still a little dull. So the same action will hurt the evolved soul more than the unevolved soul.

Now, let us apply this analogy to the animals and the vegetables. The animals are supposed to have evolved a little bit more in their consciousness than the plants. The Hindu scriptures say, "Consciousness sleeps in mineral life, dreams in plant life, awakens in animal life." In animals we see instinct functioning. Then, in the human level, we see intelligence, and finally in the superhuman - the Yogi - intuition functions. It is all the same consciousness functioning at different levels.

It is with this awareness that we say the animals feel pain more than the plants. Since we still have to eat to live, but we want to reduce the pain-giving, the violence, where should we go? To the plants. And if you want to be still less violent, you can think even further. There have been many saints in India who said, "No, I cannot even pluck an unripe fruit." They live on fruits that have already fallen from the tree. If you try to pluck an unripe apple, the tree will resist you: "No, no, don't take it; I'm not ready yet." It is still "cooking" the apple. If by force you pluck it anyway, it bleeds, it weeps. You are hurting the tree. Wait until the fruit comes off in your hand by the mere touch. Then you are truly non-violent. Moreover, after you eat the fruit, you throw the seed somewhere. That is nature's way of spreading. The fruit is your bait. "Come on, eat my flesh, but throw my seeds somewhere else. Let me spread out." You are not hurting the plant. On the other hand, you are expanding its species. You cannot do that with animals. You cannot eat the thigh of a cow and throw the head somewhere and make another cow grow.

Compassion and Moral Accountability

Where is our *karuna*, our compassion? What is happening to our hearts? If you have even once seen pictures of the young seals being killed for their fur, you will never wear fur again. In the same way, if you once saw how the animals die in the slaughterhouse, you would never want to eat meat again. Just because the killing is done by somebody else, somewhere else, does not mean that the *karma*, the responsibility, is not yours. You are contributing to their actions, and you share their *karma*.

Suppose tomorrow all the butchers were to say, "We are not going to kill for your sake anymore. If you want to eat an animal, you kill it." How many of you are ready to bring a lamb into your kitchen - the mother holding one leg, the father holding another, the son cutting it open while it screams and yells in pain, its blood splashing everywhere, all the fecal matter coming out - and then clean up all the blood and filth, cut it up and eat it? No. When it is all wrapped up in nice cellophane, with no blood, no smell, just sitting in the supermarket case, then it seems all right to you.

When people do kill the animals themselves, seeing their blood and hearing their cries, eventually their hearts forget to be compassionate. They no longer see the pain they are causing. Some so-called compassionate people think, "If you chop their heads quickly before they even realize that they are going to die, it is humane." That is not so. Even miles away, hours before the slaughter, they know. You do not have to see them, nor do they have to see you. It is direct thought transference. They know that someone is coming to kill them.

We hear of so many organizations dedicated to saving pets. Members will go to court to save the life of a cat. Yet, those same people will kill hundreds of calves and cows for their parties. What is the difference between the cat's life and the cow's life? Every day so many animals are killed for food. What is the difference? "Cruelty toward animals..." these people cry; but why have they not extended that to our lambs, to our cows?

We are destroying the hearts and souls of millions of animals. We think we can get away without facing the *karma* for this, but we cannot. The Bible says, "Thou shalt not kill;" we interpret that as thou shalt not *murder* - meaning only our fellow human beings. You can kill animals but you cannot kill a person because that is "murder." If you kill a man, you are taken to court; if you kill an animal, nobody will take you to court for that. But there is always God's court. He puts us into a bodily "prison" by creating problems within our own systems.

Why do you think that there are more people labeled insane here in the United States than anywhere else in the world? Every half hour someone goes insane. Every twenty minutes somebody commits suicide. We have the greatest number of cancer patients, the greatest number of heart patients. Why? It is our *karma* and we are paying. Whatever we do to other living beings comes back to us. That is the Nature's law. Nobody can save us from that. What you sow you have to reap. Instead of eating animals, we should learn to love them, or even to use them for good purposes, but not to kill them and eat them. When you die you have a graveyard somewhere. But, when they die, where is their graveyard? In your stomach.

We say we want a loving world, a peaceful world; but we cannot cultivate that love if negative vibrations get into us. One way in which we can bring negative vibrations into ourselves is through our food. That is why food should come to us as an offering of love. Whatever we eat should be the product of love. When I say a loving offering, I do not mean that someone cooks a nice chicken soup or broiled steak and then offers it to you lovingly. The question is, "Did the animal who died to make that steak love you?" I do not think that any animal would die lovingly for you. Will a cow come and say, "Oh, you seem to be very weak and hungry, would you like my thigh for a soup? Take it." No, you have to kill it, destroy it. In the same way, when you catch a fish, it does not come willingly. You have to cheat the fish by throwing a worm. Every time you catch a fish you are literally deceiving it. It is as if you are saying, "Come on, my friend, I will feed you." But when it comes to you, you hook it and kill it. Could you say that it is a love offering? The animals we kill hate us. If our food brings hatred, we cannot develop love.

You do not know how many thousands of animals will worship you if you become a vegetarian. You can be certain of that. A great South Indian saint Thiruvalluvar says, "If a person refrains from killing to eat, such a one will be worshipped by all the creatures of the world." It is true. Even a wild dog will wag his tail at you. The animals will feel that you are a non-violent person. Do not think that only the human beings have telecommunication. The animals have their own media, and fortunately *their* media carries the good news as well as the bad. If you have saved the life of another animal somewhere - it need not be even of the same species - the other animals will know, "You saved my brother over there."

So eating the products of violence brings a violent vibration to the mind. You are what you eat; forget not that. Your food should be a gift of love because the vibrations with which food comes to us will affect us. I will tell you a story about this - a true story.

Once, in India, a swami was invited to a rich man's house for a nice lunch. Normally, when the swami goes, a few disciples go with him. So they all went there and had a sumptuous lunch. It was served on beautiful silver plates, with silver cutlery, because the host was a very rich man. At the end of the meal, the swami blessed the man and his family, said goodbye, and left the house with his disciples.

They had been walking for about half a mile when one disciple, the youngest one, came running to the swami, "Swamiji, Swamiji, I made a terrible mistake!" The swami asked him, "What mistake is that?"

"Oh, I'm even ashamed to tell you, because I have never done anything like this before!"

"It's all right," the swami answered. "Don't worry; tell me." The disciple's hand was shaking as he pulled a silver spoon from his pocket. He said, "I took this from the man's house!" The swami smiled at him and said, "All right, you are still young, you are a beginner in spiritual practice. You will become strong as time goes on. Now, take it back and apologize; we will wait for you."

The other disciples questioned the swami: "Why were you so lenient with him? Don't you think you should be more strict?" The swami said, "No, it is not entirely his mistake."

"He stole the spoon, and you say it's not his mistake?!" Finally the swami explained, "Do you know the fellow who fed us, the rich man? He collected all that money through theft. He was formerly a banker, and he used to overcharge his customers. So, in a way, he is a thief. When he fed us with his food the vibrations of a thief also came with the food. You are all a little older and stronger, so it did not affect you. But he was affected by that vibration, and so he took the spoon."

It is a true story. I know the people involved very well. What does it mean? The fellow was a thief, and had bought the food that he served that day with money that had been gained fraudulently. The food had that vibration. If you understand this, how careful you will be about how you get your food. Not all food is clean. It should come to you in a clean way and with a good heart. So think of this in the light of the animal food that you take.

Economic and Ecological Considerations

Our human family is starving in many parts of the world. People say that there is not enough food for us all, that overpopulation is the cause. But I say that overpopulation is not the problem; rather, human greed is the problem. If we were only willing to care and share, there would be enough for everyone.

How can I say this? According to agricultural statistics, you must feed 16 pounds of grain to a steer in order to get one pound of meat; and meat has become a status symbol now in this country. The amount of grain we use to produce meat is almost equal to the amount consumed as food in the poorer countries.[5]

Another way of looking at it is this: on the average, an acre of land used for grain production gives five times as much protein as an acre used for producing meat; an acre of beans or lentils gives ten times as much protein; and an acre of vegetables, fifteen times as much protein.[6] So to feed a meat-eater, how much more land is needed! If everyone were to become a vegetarian, there would be plenty of food - and plenty of protein - for everyone. As Mahatma Gandhi used to say, "The earth has enough for everyone's need, but not enough for everyone's greed."

"But Jesus ate meat. . ."

Sometimes my Christian friends bring up the argument, "But

Jesus ate meat and fish." My answer is: Jesus walked on water; Jesus accepted crucifixion. Are you ready to do that? "Oh, I'm not like Jesus in *that* way," they say. We just choose what we want to follow. We point out great saints and sages: "He did it, she did it, why shouldn't I?"

Here is an example of why. Once the great Hindu saint Acharya Shankara was walking with his students. It was a hot day and he felt thirsty. So he stopped a person who was coming from the other direction with a pot of some liquid.

"I'm thirsty, will you give me something to drink?" The man hesitated. "Sir, what I have is not fit for you." He was carrying a kind of country liquor, called *natadi*, commonly made from the palmyra tree.

"It doesn't matter; come on, give me some," he said, and he drank it. The students suddenly found that they were thirsty, too, so they also drank from the pot. The group began moving forward, with the disciples weaving here and there, drunk. They had walked a few miles more in the hot sun when Shankara said, "I'm thirsty again."

He noticed a shop at the side of the road where a blacksmith was boiling lead in a pot. The liquid was milky and white, so he said, "You seem to be boiling some milk." Without even giving the blacksmith a chance to say anything, he took some of the liquid and drank it. Then he looked at the disciples and said, "I think all of you must be thirsty; come, drink!" They immediately realized their mistake and fell at his feet. "Now we see; we cannot imitate you in everything."

If a small plant wants to imitate a big tree and says, "I don't want any fence around me. That big fellow doesn't have any fence," what will happen? The cows will come and eat it. We should know our limitations. Let us not simply say, "Jesus did it. Moses did it." Moses spoke to God. With whom do you speak?

I once went to visit the Christian monks on the Greek island of Mt. Athos. I was surprised to find them all strict vegetarians. It reminded me of the very first thing that the Bible says about diet: "And God said, 'Behold, I have given you every herb-bearing seed, which is upon the face of the earth, and every tree, in which are fruits; for you it shall be as meat.'" (Genesis 1:29) The Dead Sea Scrolls contain some of the teachings from the time of Jesus on meat-eating: "And the flesh of slain beasts in a person's body will become his own tomb. For I tell you truly, he who kills, kills himself, and whosoever eats the flesh of slain beasts eats the body of death." And when St. Paul went out preaching he said in his letter to the Romans, "It is good not to eat flesh..." (Romans 14:21).

I have also had the opportunity to read some of the works of the 14th Century Christian saints recorded in the library of manuscripts housed at the Order of the Cross in England. Almost every one recommended pure vegetarian food and no liquor, even in the name of Eucharist. Some of them even laughed at the people who ate meat and used wine in that way. They said, "If you people want to drink, don't bring God in there. Go home and drink, but don't bring it to the altar." Why? They said, "How can you expect your mind to be clean when you are taking meat and alcohol?"

That is the reason almost every religion advocates at least some days of adherence to vegetarian diet. Whether they know the reasons or not, religious people of many different faiths stay away from animal food on auspicious days. They call it an "Ash Wednesday," or a "Good Friday." Why is it a "good Friday"? By not eating meat, you make it a good Friday, a holy day. The Chinese celebrate their New Year's Day with strict vegetarian diet. New Year's is a new beginning and they want it to be very auspicious and holy, so they stay away from meat. By staying away from meat you make a day holy. If you stay away from meat *every* day, every day will be a holy day. Consciously or not, we recognize the effect of food on the mind and know that a vegetarian diet leaves the mind more serene, more peaceful.

Two Approaches to Becoming a Vegetarian

Many people ask, "How do I go about becoming a vegetarian?" One way is to make a gradual transition to vegetarian diet. Leave off eating red meat, but continue eating fish and fowl for some time.

Then leave off the fowl, and eat only fish and eggs for some time. And then, finally, eat only vegetarian food. But if you are totally convinced of the value of becoming a vegetarian and you have strong will power, I would recommend that you drop it all right away. When you discover that something is not good for you, why not reject it?

The body which is used to the flesh food may still "demand" it. You may feel a kind of addiction, like the craving for the nicotine in cigarettes. Your cells remember it; they still have the toxins in them. So it may be difficult at first. If your body is very much saturated with toxins, you may face some headaches, even some nausea, until the toxins are purged out. If it happens that way, it certainly is not going to kill you. And there are some things that will help you, should you find yourself experiencing any uneasiness.

First of all I would recommend that you do not take any stimulants, such as coffee or tea, during this period. Why? Because the coffee brings caffeine, which is another kind of toxin, into your system. When the caffeine comes in, it invites its sister, purine, which is a toxin found in meat. Then those two call for their other sister, nicotine. I call them the I-N-E sisters. That is why, after a sumptuous meat dinner, you want a cup of coffee in one hand and an "extra millimeter longer" in the other. They all go together.

So at least for a while, try to stay away from stimulants such as coffee and tea. For anyone who might be trying to quit smoking, these things will also be helpful. Drink a lot of pure water. Take some saunas. Sunbathe if possible. Sweat a lot. All of these things will push out the toxins from your system and relieve the discomfort. When the toxins are gone, you will lose the craving for meat. Another way is simply to begin practicing the Yoga postures and breathing. I have seen many, many people who did not choose to become vegetarians consciously, but found that the habit of meat-eating fell away when they took up Yoga practice. The system becomes cleaner and more sensitive to the toxic effects of a meat diet.

Living With Non-Vegetarians

Often one member of a family will want to be a vegetarian while the others do not. You may even have to cook for meat-eating members of the family. What should you do? If they are not yet ready to understand the importance and benefit of a vegetarian diet, you should accept that. If you are the one to cook and they want you to prepare meat, you can feel, "It is my duty to provide for them; it need not upset me." If you demand that they change, you are forcing your ideas on them. Instead, let them decide for themselves that they want to change by seeing the beauty of your life. When they see you always healthy, happy and peaceful, let them ask, "What is your secret?" You can just answer, "It is because of my diet." If they are sensible they will also slowly change. Meanwhile, just give them their food. There is nothing wrong in it. It will not make you a non-Yogi or a violent person. On the other hand, it will make you a better Yogi if you do it pleasantly, with a loving heart.

Sometimes there is a tendency to become arrogant. You might feel: "Oh, I am a big Yogi now. I stopped eating meat, drinking, smoking. I am a holy person now, a pure person." You might find yourself putting others down. That is Yogic arrogance. If you really want to be a good Yogi, be more humble. Humility will bring out all of your beautiful qualities. That way you can help many people. Humility is the greatest virtue because it shows people that you have learned a lot, that you are rich in knowledge. Anything that is very light and hollow will rise up in a balance. Anything that is heavy will sink. Have you ever seen a wheat plant growing? As long as the wheat grains are raw, not yet rich with nutrition, they will stand upright, as if to say, "Here I am!" As they slowly become ripened, they become heavy and bend down. Likewise with us if we have rich, good qualities we will bow down. Do not hesitate to say to people, "I don't know." If they still demand to know your secret, you can say, "Well, because you are asking, I will tell you what I know, what I feel." Share what you have with humility.

Sometimes it is the person who does the cooking who insists that the others should eat meat, or that all the family members should eat the same thing at a meal. You can explain, "I am eating for my stomach and you are eating for yours. Although we are a family, we still have some personal things. Because we are one family, if I need to use the toilet, should you also come and sit on the toilet?" Or if another family member demands that the food you eat be the same, suggest, "Then why not the quantity also?" Another may eat one piece of toast; you may eat three pieces. Should he or she say, "We are one family; we should eat the same amount"? No; it does not make sense.

If the other one still insists, you can try a little acting. Say, "Okay, honey, to satisfy you I will eat what you want." Put it in your mouth, chew it, swallow it - and then pretend you are sick, that you are going to throw up. Just start rushing to the bathroom. . . Surely the loved one will say, "Oh, no, I can see that this food is not for you. I'm so sorry..." That is better than just saying, "I'm not going to eat *that* - I'm a ve-ge-TAR-ian. I'm pure...!" That will just create bad feelings in the family.

Occasionally, a child might be the one who wants to eat meat in a vegetarian home. Here I would say that there are many things we do not allow children to decide for themselves until they grow to a certain maturity. Until then you have a duty to bring them up along the right lines, in a way conducive to their health. Children should have freedom, but in certain areas they do not yet know what is right and what is wrong. If a child does not know how to use a knife, will you put it in those inexperienced hands just because the child cries for it? No. You are the caretaker.

It is our duty as parents to do everything possible for the sake of the children. If it is you who still eat meat and you do not want to give it up, but you want your child to be a vegetarian, probably you should make the change, at least for the child's sake. The modern way is for parents to have a glass of whiskey in one hand, a cigarette in the other, and say, "Child, I never want to see you drinking or smoking!" If you absolutely cannot set an example, at least do these things out of their sight. Remember that children are not play-things. Raising children is a big responsibility. For that we may have to change ourselves too.

Should our pets be vegetarians too?

Dogs and cats are carnivores by nature. They can live on vegetarian food, but it is not their natural diet. Just because a vegetarian diet is recommended for us, that does not mean we should try to make everyone and everything else follow it too. Certainly the meat-eaters are not trying to feed their cows meat. Then why should we try to make the dogs and cats vegetarians? It will not be bad *karma* for you to feed them their meat because you are not eating it. Your dog serves you as a watchdog or in other ways and you are taking care of it. If you have a car that runs on high octane gas, you buy high octane gas. If you have a diesel car, you should buy diesel fuel. So give your pets their own type of food; there is nothing wrong in it.

What can we do about garden pests?

Another question often asked is, "What about the insects that feed on the vegetables we are growing? Is it wrong to kill them?" You are growing the food for your use, not for theirs. If you want to be really kind to them, allot a small patch for them: "That is your area; you can eat all you want over there, but don't come here." If you feel you must forcefully remove them from your vegetables, warn them every day for three days. Each time make the warning stronger, and on the third day tell them, "This is your final warning. Those who do not leave are going to be destroyed." Then, if there are any left, you can do it. If you have given such a warning, your conscience will be clear. The insects will leave. The same principle applies to weeds; the life force will even depart from the weeds with such a warning. That is the most gentle way.

Is vegetarianism necessary for attaining enlightenment?

I am not recommending vegetarian diet because it is the only way to attain enlightenment. I advocate it because it helps you physically and mentally to make yourself more relaxed and calm, so that you can realize the spirit within sooner. It is a help, but it is not a must. If you have the capacity to control the mind, to keep it tranquil under all circumstances, you can certainly eat anything you want; you can lead any life you want. What is necessary is to keep the mind tranquil, because only in tranquility of mind can the God within you express itself, or be realized. And, generally, meat is a *rajasic* food that brings restlessness to the mind. If you have a strong mind you can probably win over that. There have certainly been saints who ate meat, but I would say that they are the exception, not the rule.

Many people tell me, "Well, I'm a vegetarian, *more or less* . . . Isn't it all right to eat a little fish or chicken every once in a while?" If you kill a chicken once in a while, it is still murder. If you eat it, you are still taking dead matter into your system, poisoning yourself. It's not that doing so will damage your life completely, but when you know these things, why should you do it even "once in a while"? In Hinduism they talk about certain vows which are called the *maha vratam* or great vows. For these, there are almost no exceptions. If the act is wrong - like stealing or killing - it is wrong. There *can* be exceptions; for example, if your life is that important to the world, and if it could be saved only by killing a chicken, fine. But that is not the same as going to a party and thinking, "Oh, I'll just eat a little; otherwise, what will they think?" If they will be that offended, act a little: "I am sorry, but my doctor asked me not to eat it because it doesn't seem to agree with me." Do not use their displeasure as an excuse for breaking your vow.

What about eggs and dairy products?

Eggs partake of the same quality as flesh. This is even true of unfertilized eggs. How do we know this? When you break an egg and leave it, it rapidly begins to decay and give off a foul odor, just as meat does. This is why vegetarians avoid eggs as well as meat.

As for milk products, if you want to be a very strict vegetarian, you can certainly do without dairy products. But milk products *do* have a different quality than meat. Some people will say, "Milk comes from the cow. If you are going to drink the milk, why not eat the flesh?" When you were a baby, you drank milk from your mother's breast, is it not? Will you then cut the flesh from your mama to eat too? It is not the same thing.

Milk products do not have the concentrated fat that meat has. Unlike eggs, if you leave milk out, it will curdle or turn sour, but it will not give of the foul smell of decaying flesh. Milk is a whole food and very *sattvic*—very conducive to a peaceful mind. Of course, if you drink too much of it, or if you do not digest it well, it will cause mucus and phlegm. And certainly we can live very well without milk products, eating only fruits, vegetables, legumes, grains and nuts.

Part II:

The Basics of
Yogic Diet

Introduction to Yogic Diet:
Knowing What, When and How to Eat

We have considered the benefits of a vegetarian diet. Is there more to be said about Yogic diet? Yes; because *what* we eat, *when* we eat, and *how* we eat are all important parts of Yoga. First of all, what do we mean by Yogic diet? The purpose of all Yoga practice is to keep the mind tranquil under all circumstances. Only in that tranquility of mind will the spirit in you express itself. When the mind is tranquil you see the God in you. All of our Yoga disciplines are to help us maintain this peacefulness. Food also plays an important part.

First, let us look at the physical side. In Yoga we acknowledge that the body and mind are intimately connected and that achieving mental poise is much more difficult when the body is not strong and well. So having robust health is often considered a helpful step in Yogic life. Here I would like to say that our food is the major cause of our physical illnesses. What we eat, we become. If we eat junk food, our bodies will have to be junked. I hear people say, "I don't have time to worry about meals. . .I usually just grab something and run." If you just "grab something," be careful, because something else will probably grab you. We should know what we are eating. In fact, if you cannot get the right food on a certain day, it would be better for you to fast for that day. We do not fall sick by not eating. As statistics show, people fall ill by overeating or by eating the wrong food, not by abstaining from food. We should take care of our food first. Let it be clean; let it give life to us. Let it contain real nutrition, not just mere taste. So a part of Yoga practice,

27

then, is dietary restriction. Eat the right toxin-free diet, in the right quantity, and in the right way.

HOW MUCH FOOD

We do not need the amount of food we sometimes think we do. People often ask me what my diet is like. I tell them that there is a continuous, relaxed state in my mind which transmits into my body also. There is no stress at all, so my body does not need much food. My fuel economy is very good. People waste a lot of energy in worrying. Our anxiety about the future drains a lot of energy. People who worry drain their batteries completely. They have to eat more. But in my case, I never drain my *prana*, my vital energy, so I can live on very little; I can even live on air alone.

Forty years ago for several months I was living on three cups of milk a day, and nothing else. During that time I was doing a lot of work in the ashram where I lived. Somehow we have come to think, "Oh, I have to eat a lot to have enough energy." No. If you do not waste your energy, you will need very little. You can even take that energy directly from the elements. Through food, we get the elements; but if we know how to take energy directly from the elements, we do not need other food at all. It is a well-known fact that in most of the Western countries people fall sick because they overeat. During World War II, there was a food shortage in many parts of Europe. At that time half of the hospitals were empty. People did not eat as much and they did not fall sick.

So we have to understand our systems. How much energy have we used up in our activities? How much do we need to replenish? There is a very simple way to know. Ask your stomach before you eat: "Tummy, are you wanting more? Have you used up what I gave you earlier?" Unless the stomach says, "Yes, I am ready," we should not eat. Many people eat for the other two "t's": "time" and the "tongue." They say, "Oh, it's 12 o'clock, I must have my lunch." Or, "What delicious pie, I must finish it." Instead, look to the third "t", the tummy. There is a beautiful saying in one of the works by the South Indian saint Thiruvalluvar which says, "The body will never need medicine if food is never taken without making sure that the stomach has digested what was given to it before." Hunger is the sign for that. Hunger is the only reliable clock for when you should eat.

Here, too, we should know what true hunger is. If your hunger "pangs" go away within a short time, then what you felt was not true hunger at all. Such hunger pangs are based on habitual eating patterns, which create a sense of false hunger. They will go away roughly within half an hour. True hunger will not go away until you have eaten something.

DIGESTIVE FIRE

I believe that proper digestive fire is much more important than a so-called balanced diet. The system knows how to balance itself. If we have that digestive fire burning within, and if we sometimes eat the wrong food, we will be able to digest it. Our digestive capacity is very important. Anything left undigested in the stomach will ferment and become acid, which gives us gas. So we should eat only when we are really hungry, and just to the limit. Then we can digest anything and everything.

If your digestion is a little weak, then you have to look for foods that have less of a mucus-producing tendency. In this regard, meat is the worst. You have to cook meat for a long time, and it takes a lot of energy to digest. It is very concentrated. Dairy products are often thought to be especially mucus-producing, and that is true if your system is weak. But even among the vegetables and fruits, some are more mucus-producing than others. These are the foods with more water content, cucumber or melon, for example. Because they cool the system, the digestive fire is immediately lowered when you eat them. Starchy foods, such as root vegetables, also take more fire to digest. The stomach is like a big oven. If you put dry sticks in it, it burns well. If you put in raw green sticks, the fire goes down. If you put a banana peel on the fire it goes down even more. So remember to eat according to the hunger and according to the fire in the stomach.

Here again, we should remember that every fireplace is different. Not all of us have the same amount of fire. The label on something may say, "This is good food; this contains so much protein," but you might not be able to digest that much. Often we see charts that say, "If you weigh this much and your height is such and such, you should eat so many calories and so much protein." But nobody looks at the stomach inside: how big it is, how much fire it has, how sluggish it is. We need to prescribe a diet for our stomachs, not for the height and weight of our bodies.

THE NINE-GATED CITY

We want to keep our bodies clean and problem-free. In order to accomplish this, we need to check what goes into them. If you want to keep a country in good shape, you establish check points - immigration entry points - at all of your borders. People must show their passports and visas before you let them in. We want to know, "Are you a good person or a criminal?" And if someone brings fruit into the country, "Is it healthy fruit or has it been bitten by insects?" Why? Because you want to preserve the health of the country. In the same way, your body is the place in which you live. In Sanskrit it is called *navadwara puri* or the "nine-gated city". It has nine major gates and millions of minor gates, such as the skin pores. Imagine that you are thirsty and want to drink some water. First, two inspectors come to check it out: the eyes. "Well, it looks clean." Then another inspector comes on the job: the nose. "Smells fine." Then the third inspector, the mouth. "Yes, it tastes okay; let it pass through."

What kind of diet will keep us healthy then? One that is plain and simple, that will keep the mind calm and serene and the body relaxed and free from toxins. It should agree with your system. It should be easy to digest. It should cost a minimum amount and require a minimum amount of time to prepare. And it should be easy to clean up after. That is the basic guideline.

Still people ask, "But can't you tell us *exactly* what to eat?" No. Don't we say, "One person's nectar is another person's poison"? Each one has to decide what is right for him or her to eat. Books may be able to give you some guidance, but ultimately you are the one who must determine what is good for you. How? By paying attention to your body. Observe your stomach. Watch its reaction to a particular food and see how it agrees with you. If it does not agree, stay away from that, or lessen the quantity. Become your own dietician. This is an important part of Yoga. You need to see what you can digest well without producing mucus or gas. Those are symptoms of indigestion. If you feel a little stuffed up or puffy, it means that you either ate the wrong food or ate the wrong quantity of food - something beyond your capacity to digest.

SOLID, LIQUID, GAS

The type of activities in which you engage are very important in determining what you should eat. This idea is almost unrecognized in Western society. The proportion of solids and liquids in your diet should go hand in hand with the type of work you do. The more physical labor you do, the more solid food you should take. If you do more mental work, you can take more liquid food and not so much solid food. A person doing hard manual labor might need three meals of solid food a day; whereas a desk worker who is mostly sitting and thinking should not eat more than one solid meal a day to keep in good health. People who are mostly meditating, or doing things with complete ease, can take more energy from the air itself. From solid, to liquid to gas: if the need is for physical energy we take food from a solid source; if the need is mental, from liquid; and if the need is spiritual, then from a gaseous source. Children who are growing need quite a lot of physical energy to make their bodies grow well, so they could eat solid food quite often.

WHEN TO EAT

When we eat in relation to when we expend energy is also very important. We should finish eating at least two hours before sleeping, and the evening food should be light. If you go to bed with undigested food in the stomach, some of your energy will go into digesting and you will not get a very good rest. The mid-day meal could be heavier because you will have plenty of time to digest, and you will be using the energy you get from that food later on. But first it is best to rest quietly for a while after a heavy meal. Taking time for digestion is very important. In India we have a saying, "When the stomach is full, the brain is dull." After eating heavy food you yawn, you cannot think well. This is because you need circulation in the brain to think and the circulation has gone down to the stomach. If you force the blood to come to the brain, then the stomach will suffer. If your work does not allow you time to rest after lunch, then have a lighter lunch and an earlier dinner.

The biggest surprise for many people who are learning about Yogic diet is the Yogic approach to breakfast. People often think that having a big meal first thing in the morning is important because they will need the energy for their work. On the contrary, when we first wake up, the digestive fire is not that strong; it is still partly sleeping. So the morning food should be light.

There is a Yogic saying that if you eat once a day you are a Yogi; twice a day, you are a *bhogi*; and three times a day, a *rogi*. What does it mean? A Yogi is a spiritual, well-balanced person. *Bhoga* means enjoyment, so if you want to just enjoy the world, eat twice a day. And *roga* means sickness; if you eat three times a day, you will probably fall sick very often.

MAKE CHANGES SLOWLY

We must decide what is best for our systems, but we do not need to be fanatics. Go slowly. Maybe you have decided that white bread is not good for you, that it is made from white flour, which is good for gluing up posters and will glue up your intestines as well. In that case, if you can buy whole grain bread, fine, do it. But if you go home and immediately toss out all the white flour products in your home, your family might go wild. Instead, know the direction in which you want to go and then proceed slowly, gently. Poison is poison, whether it is a little or a lot; but some poisons will kill you immediately, while others harm you more slowly. Think of where you are, who you are with and your capacity - and then use your common sense.

Suppose you go to the home of a good friend or a relative and you are served white bread or something similar made with all love for you. You need not immediately say, "Hey, I'm a Yogi; I can't eat this rubbish!" The harm to your friend's feelings is worse than the harm the bread would do to you. Take a taste; act as if you are really enjoying it, and eat more of the vegetables. You have to judge what is more important in a situation. But, if you are really keen in improving your diet, there is always a way. If you want to avoid caffeine, but you still want a hot drink like coffee, you can take decaffeinated coffee or one of the many cereal beverages. Where there is a will, there is a way.

HOW TO EAT

How we eat our food is also very important. Do not use your mouth as a funnel to get the food to the stomach as quickly as possible! How often we see people shovel it in and the next minute it is gone. We should be using all of our 32 teeth to chew, and we should be chewing well. As I mentioned before, digestion actually begins in the mouth; there are digestive enzymes in the saliva itself. The saying, "Well begun is half done," can be applied to the digestion also.

I would also recommend that you take care to eat at a time when your body and mind are well relaxed. If you are upset, angry or agitated for any reason, it is better not to eat at that time. You will literally be poisoning your system. It is also better not to prepare food for yourself or for others at such a time, because those vibrations will go into the food you are cooking and affect those who eat it. It is best to prepare food with a calm mind, and to sit silently for a few moments before you begin eating, taking some time to consciously relax the body and let go of any distracting or disturbing thoughts in the mind. A short prayer of dedication or thanksgiving might be said during this time, or you might just want to spend a moment in silent meditation.

Generally, I would suggest that you take your meals in silence. It is best to concentrate on the food while you are eating it. You will digest better and enjoy your meal more. How many times do we get so engrossed in conversation that we do not even taste the food? If there is conversation, it should be light and pleasant. A "business" lunch or dinner does not do justice to either the business or the meal. The business deal will be sounder if your mind is only on the business and if part of your energy is not going into digestion. And your stomach will be happier if you focus all of your attention on your food while you are eating. This kind of awareness will also help a lot if you tend to have a problem with eating more than you should.

The Properties of Food

In Yogic thinking, everything in nature is divided into three groups according to the three *gunas* or qualities mentioned before: *sattva, rajas* and *tamas. Sattva* is the tranquil state, *rajas* the very active state, and *tamas* the state of inertia or dullness. One of the main scriptures of Yoga, the *Bhagavad Gita,* speaks at great length on the qualities of different diets. Foods that are close to their natural state - not very spicy, sour or hot - are considered to be *sattvic.* These include fruits, nuts, milk products, vegetables (raw and cooked), cooked grains and peas or beans. When the same products are mixed with a lot of spices and become sour or hot, they become *rajasic.* That means they create a restlessness in the mind. Since our main goal is to keep the mind in a tranquil state, we use the aid of everything in our daily lives to retain a state of health and tranquility. *Rajasic* food also includes meat and other flesh food. They make us active in a restless, sometimes aggressive, way. All foods that are old, overcooked, or very cold, come under the *tamasic* category. That would also include any food that has been cooked and then kept for a long time or food that is moldy.

The manner in which we eat can also make the resulting state of body and mind *sattvic, rajasic* or *tamasic.* For example, if we do not chew a *sattvic* food well, so that it can be well assimilated, it will ferment within the body and can cause *tamas* or the quality of inertia. Or, if we overeat or eat right before going to sleep, we will also become *tamasic.*

According to *ayurveda,* the ancient Indian system of medicine, foods can also be divided according to the effect they have on the body. The categories are: *vata* or wind-producing; *pitta* or bile-producing; and *kapha,* mucus-producing. All foods and herbs can be categorized that way. Some of each quality will be found in every food, but one of the three qualities will be predominant. Take, for example, the mucus-producing category: all pumpkins and gourds have a lot of water, and so they are cooling and produce mucus. However, this does not mean that they are not good food. If your body produces more bile, you may need exactly those foods to counteract the bile and bring a balance. Or you might need to take a food like eggplant, which is wind-producing. In *ayurveda*, you are helped to maintain a balance by taking foods of the categories other than the one which is predominant in you.

This philosophy goes even deeper. The wind-producing food is associated with the element air, the bile-producing with fire, and the mucus-producing with water. Everything in nature comes from the five elements. Moreover, each element comes from the one before it: from ether, comes air; from air, comes fire; from fire, comes water; and from water, comes earth. That is why I say you can convert any one food into all the elements you need for health if your system is pure, strong and subtle. There are people - mostly great saints and sages - who are able to live on air alone. You can experiment a little with this yourself. If you practice a lot of *pranayama* -the Yogic breathing - your physical food consumption will go down. You will not feel the need to eat as much because you will be getting your nourishment from the *prana* itself.

Mono-Diet and Food Combining

The idea of a mono-diet is often used in the naturopathic approach to healing. Mono-diet means eating only one thing at a time, rather than putting a lot of different foods into the stomach at the same time: one type of fruit, or one vegetable, or one grain, for example. If you eat this way, your body will digest the food more easily and assimilate it much better.

Therefore I suggest that if you want to eat some fruit, eat just one kind of fruit at a time. Eat one - or even four - apples, but do not mix them with cantaloupe. If you are eating carrots, eat only carrots for that meal. Your stomach will be grateful to you because it will have just one thing to do; digestion will be much quicker and easier. This is because each food takes a different amount of time to digest and utilizes different enzymes.

Digestion is similar to cooking in this way. When you want to

35

make a vegetable stew, you do not put everything into the pot at once. You put the roots first, later the broccoli, and much later, the leafy green vegetables. So think of the stomach as a cooking pot. Sometimes I have seen people eating steamed vegetables with fried food. The fried things will take a longer time to digest, whereas the steamed vegetables take much less time.

If you really feel you need a little more variety, then eat two or three things together that would be digested in a similar way and in the same amount of time. For instance, it is especially helpful not to have cooked and raw food at the same meal. And as a general rule, I would advise that if you are eating solid food, you should stick to solids; if you are drinking, have only liquids. This idea, too, is almost unknown in the West. We often see people drinking coffee or wine while eating meat and vegetables, or ending a meal with a beverage. Even water should not be taken during a meal of solids. It will dilute the digestive juices. Liquids should be taken an hour or two before or after solid food. If you get thirsty while you are eating, it is because you are not chewing enough before swallowing. If you chew well, you will not feel thirsty. I often say that you should drink your solids and eat your liquids. How? When eating, chew the food well until the solids break down and become a liquid, mixing completely with your saliva. When drinking, mix the liquids well in your mouth and swallow them slowly, as you do when you chew.

Another bad habit many people have is drinking milk with other food. Milk is a whole food in itself and should be taken alone. Perhaps if you really want something else, you could have a banana with it. Citrus should never be taken at the same time as milk. This sounds like common sense; no one would pour orange juice into a glass of milk. But think how common it is for people to have a breakfast that includes orange juice in a glass and milk in a bowl of cereal. We should think of how all these principles might be applied.

Today there is also a lot of concern about how to get enough bulk in one's diet. Food that is eaten whole and raw has a lot of bulk in it. For example, when you eat a whole raw apple you get bulk from the cellulose coating. Almost everything should be eaten with the husk on it: vegetables, fruits, beans, even grains. We spend money to take the bran out of the wheat for white flour products; then we spend money to buy extra bran to supplement our diet. If we eat products in their whole state, we will get plenty of bulk.

There is another advantage to eating raw food. We consume much less of the same food when it is not cooked. Take cauliflower, for example. The average person could not eat even half of a raw cauliflower. But if it were cooked, the same person could easily eat the entire vegetable. By eating uncooked food, we save food, we get more bulk, and at the same time we save time and energy in preparing it. I often say that the day human beings learned to cook their food was the day they began laying the foundations for the hospitals.

Food and Pain

When we overeat or eat the wrong thing, we may experience stomach ache, headache, pain, or nausea and vomiting. If you put toxins into the system, they will accumulate and cause you pain. Why? They are saying, "Somehow you accumulated us. We won't be helpful to you, so please get us out of here and remember not to put any more in." If it were not for the headache, you would torture the body more and more. Without the stomach pain, you would keep on gobbling. It is the physical pain that brings us this message. The body is telling you, "I have had enough; you are torturing me too much. Stop it." The pain itself is an alarm, a warning.

But what do we often do? We kill the pain that brings the message. First you put in all the steak, hotdogs, beer and junk food. Then the body cries out: "My God, I am not made for this. I am a simple thing. I just want simple, plain vegetables. Why are you putting all this junk into me? I cannot take it anymore." Instead of listening, we say, "How dare you tell me that? If you continue to give me this message, not only will I keep on eating as I please, but I am going to destroy you with a pain killer." It is as if the fire alarm in your home goes off and you wake up and say, "Hey, you miserable alarm!", and then get up, cut the wire and go back to sleep. Would you do that? No. You would get up and find out what was setting off the alarm. Likewise, we should be looking for the cause of our pain.

Fasting

Fasting is a natural process. Animals do it. Almost every spiritual and folk tradition in the world talks about it. It is only in recent times that people seem to have come to fear it and to feel that they must eat every day no matter what. The body is like any other factory. You make the machines work all week, then you give them some down time for rest or cleaning and overhauling. In the same way, even if we are eating the right food, our digestive systems need a little rest from their ordinary routine. Actually, it is more like a "break" than a rest, because the system takes advantage of that time to burn up any toxins or excess fat that might have been inadvertently put into it. It overhauls itself and gets ready for the next day's work. If we eat the proper foods and have only a light supper, our system has a mini-fast every night during which it gets cleaned up and the stomach gets some rest. Unfortunately, our heavy dinners and late evening meals often prevent that, and longer fasts of a day or more become advisable at such times. For a healthy person with a reasonably good diet, I recommend one day of fasting a week. It can be any day that is convenient for you, but stick to the same day each week - perhaps a weekend day so that you can have more quiet time. This will take care of any small problems in your system before they can become big problems.

If fasting is good for healthy people, it is even more important for those who are weak or sick. When your body is sick, your stomach is also sick. By eating, you make your sick stomach work more. Instead, allow it to rest and heal. There is a saying in Sanskrit, "Fasting is the best medicine." Normally, when you are ill, you do not feel much like eating. So it is more natural not to eat at such times. If you want to help cure almost any ailment, stay away from food until you feel the symptoms subside and experience real hunger again. When you give that rest to your system, your vital energy inside will act as an inner doctor to burn up the toxins that have created the sickness. This applies also to any extra fat or toxins, minor physical problems, and aches and pains in the body. When you fast, you eliminate the toxins, digest the undigested food, assimilate the extra fat and come back to normal health.

The following are some general guidelines on fasting. If you have any doubts or questions on undertaking a fast for yourself, it would be best to consult an expert in the field.

WHAT TO TAKE DURING YOUR FAST

In my experience, the best way to fast is to just drink plain water. On certain religious holidays, some people even fast without water. In India, when devotees fast without water and they feel thirsty, they put a few peppercorns in their mouths, bite them gently, and when the saliva comes, they swallow it. But if you are fasting for health reasons, I would recommend drinking plenty of water. If that is too difficult for you, then take juice diluted with water. I hear of people drinking carrot juice four or five times a day on their fast. Each glass of carrot juice takes six or seven carrots to make, so in a day you might be consuming thirty or forty raw carrots in the form of juice. I would not recommend this. One should take fruit juices, such as grape or orange juice, that are more watery. Watermelon is also excellent to have while fasting.

ENEMAS AND PURGATIVES

It is good to take enemas regularly once or even twice a day while you are fasting. This is because the system gets heated when you fast; even the colon develops heat. Since the moisture from the waste matter will then be absorbed back into the system, it is better to eliminate the wastes. Even before beginning the fast, you might want to take a purgative to clean the bowels. I would recommend castor oil or another natural type of purgative. This is especially important if you are fasting to cure an infection. Any inflammation in the body will be aggravated, and any swelling will become more painful, if the stomach or colon is still heavy with the undigested, fermented matter.

SYMPTOMS OF CLEANSING

You should know in advance that you may experience some unpleasant symptoms while fasting. If you know that they are all signs of cleansing, you will welcome them and not become frightened. The symptoms come because toxins are being removed from the organs, glands and tissues into the bloodstream, and are then being eliminated through the perspiration, breath, urine and solid wastes. It is similar to cleaning a carpet in your home. Before you disturb the carpet, the house might look beautiful and clean. But the minute you start moving and shaking the rug, all kinds of dust and dirt come out.

The same thing happens while fasting; all the toxins come out. You may experience a headache because of it. If so, drink more water. If you feel nauseated, drink a lot of water and then throw it right up. I have heard people say, "Oh, whenever I stop eating I get nauseated, I get a headache. So I *must* eat." That is incorrect. These are signs that you are cleaning out the body. If you stick with it, the headache and nausea will go away. Sometimes you will suddenly feel that you have lost all your strength. That is fine. Do not do anything strenuous for a while, but continue the fast. The tongue will get coated, and your breath and saliva may smell and taste foul. That is because the whole "rug" is being shaken all the dirt is being tossed up. I recommend that you sunbathe if possible during your fast so that you will perspire and cleanse more. Sunbathing is like a very mild sauna that does not stress the system. Deep breathing is also an excellent way to help eliminate the toxic material more quickly. The Yoga *kriyas* are also good: especially nasal cleansing with water and the stomach wash.[1]

HOW LONG TO FAST

How long you should fast depends on how much toxic material you have accumulated in your system. It might take two days to eliminate, or four, or ten. There are very definite signs that let you know when you have finished, however. You will feel light. Your saliva will become clean, clear and sweet-tasting, like spring water. Your tongue will no longer be coated. Your eyesight will be sharper. All of the senses will become more alert, and you will not have any feeling of dullness or drowsiness. An amazing feeling of strength will come. You may not have the strength to do physical work, but you will feel like running, like flying!

At one time I was living at a place of pilgrimage in South India where the shrine is located one thousand steps up, at the very top of a hill. I fasted for a number of days, and after the fourth day I felt as if I could fly up the hill. When you get these signs, you know that it is time to break the fast. At that point you will feel a hunger that will not go away until you eat something. That is the time to break the fast.

HOW TO BREAK A FAST

How you break a fast - and with what - is very important. I would even say that the way in which you break a fast is more important than the fast itself. If you fast for a few days, it is best to take the same amount of time to completely return to your normal diet. For example, if you fast for four days, take four days to break the fast, starting with lighter foods in small quantities. If your fast is longer, the same basic principle applies: take some time to gradually work up to eating denser foods and larger quantities again.

Here are some general guidelines: first have a liquid such as apple juice, or diluted juice if you have been fasting on water alone. The next step would be to have a thin yogurt or other semi-solid. You can cut up some pieces of cucumber, and some fresh corriander leaves if you can get them, and add this to the yogurt. For the next stage you might have something even more solid, perhaps a light cooked cereal such as cream of wheat. Then progress to steamed vegetables. As you come out of the fast, slowly, slowly increase the density of your food until you are back to your normal diet. Never break a fast with a big meal or heavy food.

Often people can fast easily, but when the time comes to break the fast, they feel compelled to pounce on any and all food that comes within reach. This is where you will need strict control over the tongue. If you cannot control the tongue, it is better not to fast. Why? Because fasting is a reconditioning of the body. Every part of the system will become more delicate, more sensitive. It is similar to overhauling an automobile engine. After an engine has been rebuilt, there is a breaking-in period: in first gear you should go only ten miles an hour; in second gear, only twenty miles an hour; in third gear, only forty miles an hour - for at least the first thousand miles. The engine must get used to working again. When you have reconditioned the body by fasting, you cannot run it at breakneck speed the following day. I see many people who fast for ten days, eat anything for two months, then fast for another ten days. This is very unhealthy for the body, and for the mind as well. If you cannot break your fast carefully, it is much better not to fast at all.

FASTING AND THE MIND

There is a higher significance to fasting also. Fasting helps to calm the mind. Mastering the body and senses will lead you to mastery of the mind. The body and senses themselves are never unruly. They are simply instruments. It is the mind that drives the senses. When the mind is not connected to the senses - in sleep, for example - they do not do anything. Even when you are awake, it often happens that you do not hear people when they call you because you are deeply engrossed in something. Why? The ears are always open, but in this case your mind is somewhere else. The senses are all gateways to the mind, instruments through which the mind functions to experience things. When you gain mastery over the senses, such as the tongue in this case, you are indirectly gaining mastery over the mind. As mentioned before, that is one of the reasons that fasting is so often associated with spiritual and religious observances. So if you would like to have more control over your mind, fasting can help you to achieve it.

Compulsive Eating

Many people suffer from the compulsion to overeat and seek to develop the will power to overcome this problem. Developing such will power is the entire purpose behind all of the Yoga practices. We want to have the control to use our will in the way we want. The best way to develop such will is to apply it to smaller things first. Start with something you feel you could easily accomplish. If you take something that is a big problem for you and immediately try to develop will power in that area, you may fall down and lose your confidence. It can put more negativity into the mind and drain the will. That is because you are taking on a task beyond your present capacity.

In order to understand how to train the will, we should look at how an animal trainer works with a valuable horse. Before the horse is expected to pull a heavily loaded cart, it is trained to simply walk on the road. Then it is made to walk on the road with a small weight on its back. Probably two wheels will be added next; then a little more weight, then an empty four-wheeled cart. Then the trainer will gradually increase the weight in the cart. That way the horse gains confidence. "Oh, is that all? I can certainly do that." While it is in such a cooperative mood, the horse will not even notice if a little more weight is added.

Our minds are also like that. A positive feeling, or self-confidence, is what you call "will." It is not something you have to - or even can - go and get from somewhere outside of you. Apply it little by little, always at a level where you feel positive and confident. For example, say you want to go on a fast. Before you overdo and fast for one whole week, just say, "Okay, for one day I am going to miss my lunch." You might think, "Oh, that's easy; anybody can do that!" Fine, do it. Then a week or two later, maybe go for a whole day with just a few glasses of juice. If you have confidence in doing that, then a week later, take just as many cups of water as you want for one day, but no juice. Keep up the confidence in yourself. This is the most important thing.

What I say may be enough advice for some people. But if you cannot change by yourself, you may need outside help to do it. Never feel that you *must* do it all by yourself. If it seems too much for you to do alone, seek the help of others.

OVERWEIGHT
If you are one of the many people who worry a lot about being

overweight, know that the worry itself will make you overweight. A heavy mind will make the body heavy. If you make your mind heavier due to anxiety about being overweight, your body will become heavier still. Most people eat more when they worry. The more you think of weight, the more you will create weight, one way or another. As you think, so you become. If you keep on saying, "I overeat; I must not overeat. I overeat; I must not overeat," you will certainly overeat. The best thing for you to do is to forget about it; then you will not do it. So to start with, even if the body is on the heavy side, keep the mind light. That is the first thing. Without the worry, you might even be able to make some healthy changes in your diet.

A lot of benefit could come from doing the Yoga practices regularly - the postures, the breathing and the cleansing practices, or *kriyas*. Especially helpful would be *agnisara* (the fire breath), *nauli* (stomach churning) and *bhastrika* (the bellows breathing)[2]. *Sarvangasana* (the shoulder stand) and *matsyasana* (the fish pose) will also help a lot in bringing balance to the thyroid gland which regulates the metabolism.[3] If you become adept at these practices, whatever you eat will be completely digested. There will not be any fat accumulating in the body. All of the practices in general will help a lot, especially if there is some sort of deficiency in the glands. The whole body can be affected if the glands are weak. If you rebuild the glands, the entire system will not get shaken by a problem in one area.

TO THOSE HEAVYSET BY BIRTH

If you are heavyset by nature, and believe that you must be thin, then you are buying the brainwashing of the business and advertising people. All kinds of things are sold to reduce your weight. Who says that you should weigh only so much? Each body is different. A horse is a horse; a deer is a deer. Both are very beautiful. Should one wish to be the other? Human constitutions also vary. Your make-up depends on who your father is, who your mother is, what your mother ate, what kind of elements she attracted to build up your body. If anyone is going to refuse your love because you weigh a few pounds more than some of the models in the magazines, then you should say goodbye to that person. As long as you are healthy, you should not worry. In fact, if you are constitutionally heavy and you starve yourself in order to reduce your weight, you will only weaken your health.

I come across many women in this situation. They feel that in order to be in style or to be popular, they must be slim or even skinny and bony. It has become the fashion that unless you are slim, you are not attractive and others will not even want to look at you. The first thing I would tell anyone caught in this trap is to shed this unhealthy notion. If a person is going to look at your flesh and bones, he or she must certainly be a butcher. Only butchers are interested in flesh, bone and skin. The minute a butcher sees an animal, he or she mentally weighs it: how much flesh can I get, what kind of nice hide can I get? If a man or woman does not want to look at you, shun him or her. They are butchers then. They are interested only in your flesh. They are not interested in your qualities. The body is simply a vehicle. It can be long and sleek, or it can be round and compact. It can even be "ugly" - with some dents and scratches, or a missing fender - and still take you farther than some of the shiny new cars just coming off the assembly line.

Of course we all know that underneath, the so-called beauties can be as ugly as scorpions and as poisonous as snakes. A cobra appears to be very beautiful - shiny, slim and dancing - but there is a deadly poison within. Therefore, let us learn to look beyond the external beauty and appreciate the real beauty that lies within. Everyone would agree with this; but do we practice it? These are not new ideas. They are repeated over and over again. A well-known saint of South India named Avvayar presents this idea beautifully. She says that the hair, dress and face powder will not really make a person beautiful. What will? The wisdom that dawns through your tranquility of mind. She is talking about Yoga. Yogic beauty is the real beauty, she says. It lies in the heart. People should learn to look at the beauty of the heart and mind first. Anyway, who says a fat person is ugly? If God hated fat bodies, certainly it would have been no trouble to make them all slim.

PRACTICAL HINTS

If you *are* overweight, here is a practical hint for reaching and maintaining the weight that is proper for your constitution. You do not need to purposely reduce the quantity of food you eat. It will automatically be reduced if you just chew your food well. Chew it until it becomes liquified in your mouth. You will find that half the amount you were eating before will now be enough. And, if possible, eat more leafy green vegetables.

If the habits are not too ingrained, another way to work on this compulsion is to analyze and train the mind. Ask the mind, "What are you gaining by overeating? Can't you see that you are not going to solve your problems this way? You are hiding from them behind the food. And not only that, you are adding more problems besides. If the mind does not want to cooperate, there is another way for it to learn. Relax and let yourself eat as much as possible. Simply eat as much as you can. Eat more and more. Give yourself full permission to do this. Eat until you throw up naturally. Eat until you get completely disgusted with it. If it is just one food that you eat compulsively, do this with that one food - ice cream, or bread or whatever it is. You will reach a point where the mind will say, "I cannot touch it anymore." So either discuss the problem with your mind and convince it to change, or allow it to get so thoroughly disgusted that it is willing to change on its own.

As a final point, I would remind you that though we use the term "overeating", you can never really overeat. If you did "overeat," you would throw up immediately. The stomach would take care of it. Usually we overestimate our eating out of anxiety. Even if you eat very little on a given day, you may still worry that you are overeating. So know that the problem here is in the mind, and that the solution is in the mind also. Change the mind first, and a change in the body will follow.

Substance Addiction

We become addicted to substances that stimulate our systems. Overly spicy food, coffee, tea, alcohol and drugs all seem to stimulate us, even though some of them may technically be called depressants. All of these may pick us up for a while; but later on we drop down to a level even lower than the one at which we started. With continued usage, our systems become weaker and weaker and we become more and more addicted to the substances to pick us up again. At first, one sip of beer would have pepped you up for a whole day; then slowly one bottle is needed, then two bottles, then a case. It is because the body becomes weaker, and you need a stronger dose. The same is true of sleeping pills and tranquilizers. With time, you need more and more to achieve the same effect.

If we want to get out of these addictions, we have to strengthen the body and mind. Some of these substances may appear to strengthen us, but they do not. Many people believe that these substances help them to think. When they get into some problem or when they are searching for an idea, and the solution does not come, they pick up their cigarettes or their cocaine. Immediately they think, "Ah, I got it!" That is because the stimulant accelerates the body and mind - but only for a while. Then it drops them down again. There are some rock singers who roar at the top of their lungs. Where do they get the energy? From drugs. But if you see them afterwards, they are like wounded animals; you cannot even go near them. I know many of them. That is not real energy or real strength. Strength can only come from proper health, not from external things brought into the body.

You may say, "Yes, we know these things are bad for our health, but we have gotten used to them; we are addicted, how can we get out of it?" Here Yoga will help a lot. If a person practices Hatha Yoga - the Yoga postures and breathing - he or she can eliminate all the toxins from his or her body. Once the toxins are gone, the craving will be gone too. For example, someone who smokes a lot may realize that smoking is harmful and want to quit; but the craving is still there. It is as if there were two people in one body. There is the person who does not want to smoke anymore, and the one that does. Who is that "other person" who has the craving? It is the body which is already filled with nicotine. In other words, the nicotine that has already gone into you wants more nicotine. That is what you call craving.

If you want to get rid of these cravings, you need to push out the addictive substances - the toxins - that are already in you. This applies to any craving, any addiction: smoking, drinking, overeating, drugs. Simply start practicing Hatha Yoga and very soon you will see the craving getting weaker and weaker, eventually going away by itself. There are hundreds of proofs of this among my students. What happens is that the postures apply a gentle pressure in all the different areas of the body where the toxins are lodged, releasing them. As you come out of the postures, the pressure is relieved and the released toxins go into the bloodstream and get eliminated through the breath. The pressure also tones and strengthens the endocrine glands and nerve centers. The Yoga postures and breathing offer the best way to eliminate toxins.[4]

Diet and Healing

If you have had an injury, an illness or surgery, you should be especially careful to take only clean, simple, toxin-free food. Avoid coffee, tea or other stimulants. If you do this, and relax well, you will be healed very quickly. I know of many, many instances of this. Here are a few examples.

Some time ago, when I was still living at my Guru's ashram in India, a woman who used to come there found out that she needed to have surgery to remove a large tumor. She asked me to oversee her convalescence. After the operation, she went to a relaxed place in the mountains with a nurse to attend to her. She ate only very clean, simple food and, although the nurse did not even want her to get up for a month, I soon had her walking daily in the fresh air. After ten days, she started doing Yoga postures. To her doctors' amazement, she was completely healed within one month.

Another notable case was that of my maternal uncle. He was always very strict with his diet, and never took coffee or tea. He was once in a very bad automobile accident, during which he received a large puncture wound in the head. The doctors at the hospital did what they could, and told him that he was not to go out for at least a month, until the wound was healed. To their surprise his head was completely healed within ten days. Not only was he a strict vegetarian, but he had never taken alcohol, coffee or even tea in all of his life. In such cases, healing is many times faster than when the body is burdened with toxins.

Here is one more example. Once a radio announcer who was looking for a cure for his many allergies told me: "I am allergic to almost everything. The doctor told me not to eat this, not to touch that. And he gave me all of these pills. I don't know what to do. What do you think?" I said, "Add one more allergy to your list: pill allergy." He was worried about what would happen to him if he stopped taking all the pills. I told him, "Nothing will happen to you if you just follow a proper Yogic diet." I also had him do some Yogic breathing. He was quite heavy, so I did not even ask him to do the Yoga postures, just the breathing. Within ten days he was a thoroughly changed person. So you do not need to be allergic. Instead, take care not to fill your body with toxic material. Build up its natural strength. The allergies will disappear. They will become allergic to you!

Vitamins

I am often asked for my thoughts about taking vitamins. Taking the vitamins we need directly from the foods we eat is much better and more natural than taking them in the form of pills. But if the food you eat itself lacks the vitamins it should have because of the conditions under which it was grown, then there is no harm in supplementing your diet. You should not take too many however. When we consume large quantities of vitamins, we are mostly consuming money. The body can assimilate only so much of a vitamin, and what it cannot assimilate gets eliminated.

A lot of the benefit can be psychological too. For a long time doctors were saying, "Vitamin C cures colds." Many, many people thought that it was curing their colds. Now it is said, "Vitamin C does not cure colds." So it can be your own feeling of "Ah, I took Vitamin C; now I will be well!" that cures you.

Some Simple Remedies

I was trained in homeopathy and nature cure, and practiced homeopathy when I was in Sri Lanka. I am often asked whether Yogic diet can help with various simple health problems, and many people have had very good results from the suggestions I have given. By experimenting, you can learn to take care of many of your own ailments. Of course, in acute cases, it is always good to trust your doctor and his or her treatment. But for more simple problems, here are a few remedies. If you are interested, you can learn many more from naturopathic doctors and other natural health practitioners.

SORE THROAT REMEDY

If the sore throat was caused by excessive use of your vocal cords, there is probably inflammation, and you must stop using them as much as possible. Give the inflammation time to heal. If, on the other hand, it is due to some kind of mucus problem, such as most so-called colds and congestion, then you can take a mucus-free diet as a remedy. To help relieve the soreness while it is healing, make a paste out of honey and ordinary ground black pepper, mixing them in whatever proportion you like. If it is too hot, use more honey; if it tastes too sweet, put in more pepper. Put some of the paste on your finger and rub it into the inside of the throat and all around the affected area. A lot of saliva will be produced. You can either swallow it or spit it out. This will help heal the inflammation and improve the health of your vocal cords.

SESAME OIL BATH FOR ARTHRITIS AND RHEUMATISM

Here is another simple health secret from a natural source. In

India most people do this regularly, but the practice is almost unknown in the West. It is to apply sesame oil all over the body, leave it on for half an hour and then wash it off. The oil could be applied to the hair and scalp also. This provides a complete lubrication for the body, and will itself take care of many ailments. It helps to take away the toxins from arthritis and rheumatic troubles, and should be done at least once a week.

NATURAL SOAPS

I would recommend that you avoid using soap as much as possible. Soap is made from caustic soda, which dries the skin. Even if oil is added to the soap, the caustic soda is still there. If you have very oily skin, you can wash with a paste of chick pea (garbanzo bean) flour. Just apply it to the body, let it dry and then rinse it off. Or use yogurt as a cleansing agent; it is very good for your health. Another cleansing paste can be made of fine mung bean powder and water. Even if your body is thoroughly soaked in oil, this paste will take it all away without harming the skin. If your skin is not oily, and you do the oil bath mentioned above, you do not even need to use soap; just shower and towel away the excess oil. The skin will remain moist. This is much more effective than using commercial creams.

Food and Yoga Practice

For the full-time, serious student of Yoga, diet takes on another significance. The fifth limb of Raja Yoga is *pratyahara* or sense control. The tongue is the most powerful of the senses, and the most difficult to control. It has two functions: eating and talking. The Indian saint Ramalinga Swamigal advises that, "If a spiritual seeker is interested in food and eating, all of his spiritual practices will be like so many things thrown into a river. The benefits will all be washed away." Without control of the tongue you can forget about spirituality; you will not be able to control any of the other senses. All of the senses, even the sexual urge, can be controlled if you control your tongue.

How much time we waste constantly thinking of ice cream and pizza. In ashrams in India they serve the same food every day. The seekers there need not even bother to ask what the menu is each day. As long as it is good for the stomach, it will do. Saint Ramalinga says, "It does not matter what you feed me, Lord. When I am hungry, whatever comes to me, whatever is offered, let me just eat. I only want to serve You. I do not even want to look at what is offered. Whatever it is, I will simply put it in my mouth, chew it, swallow it, and be finished. I will say, 'Okay, body, I have paid you your due, now don't bother me anymore.'" This is the attitude of a true spiritual seeker. If one day there is nothing to eat, fine. "Well, Lord, probably that is your will for me today."

The monks in India have some very simple rules about food. Right at noon they are to take their begging bowl, go in front of a householder's house and stand there "for the time it would take a capable person to milk a cow." (When these rules were thought of there were no clocks or watches.) They are to simply say once, *"Bhavati, bhiksham dehi"* - "please give me some alms." If there is no response, they may go to another house, but with a limit of seven houses. If they get enough at the first house, they need not go further. But if they do not get anything even after seven houses, then they take it that the Goddess did not want them to eat that day. And that is not all. If they do get some food, they are to go to the river bank, sit down and look here and there to see if anyone is around. If they see one or two people, they offer them as much as they want to eat. If there is anything left over, the monk may eat it. If five people come and eat it all, their attitude is: "I see, God came in five different forms and ate everything. I have been blessed, and He wants me to fast today."

I am not saying that you should take up a begging bowl tomorrow. But you should have that attitude, "Yes, God will give me whatever is necessary." If you are really serious about the Yogic path, keep your food simple and just eat it and be done with it.

When you are fasting, keep the mind well occupied with things other than food. Do more Yoga practices; do not even give yourself time to think about food. That is real fasting. You are then keeping your mind away from food also. If you keep your body away from food but still fill the mind with it, you are not really fasting.

It is especially important to keep the stomach light if you want to meditate. Meditation means focusing the mind on one point with total concentration, and for this you need all your energy. When you eat, at least part of your energy immediately rushes to the stomach to digest the food. If you eat a lot, you will need all of your energy to go there. If you try to meditate, your energy gets confused: "What should I do now? Digest the food or help him meditate? Well, probably he can use his mind later but the food should not be left undigested so I'll go there first." Then the brain becomes dull and you feel like sleeping instead of meditating. Again, this is why the tradition for so many religious holidays is to fast or eat lightly, so that you can spend your energy in prayer and meditation. If you want to be en-light-ened, keep the stomach light.

If your system is pure and strong, you will be able to digest anything. You will be immune to all the minor ailments and allergies. Your digestive fire will also be strong. Sometimes people tell me, "I have been following your suggestions and have made my diet very simple and pure. But instead of becoming stronger, I have become overly sensitive. If I go off my diet even a little, I immediately develop some physical symptoms or fall sick. What is happening to me?" To this I must say, that is the problem with Yoga! If a glass of water is already dirty and you throw in more dirt, it will scarcely be noticeable. Or if you put on your dirty jeans and go do some greasy job, the new dirt will not show. But if you start with clean, pure water, even a speck of dirt will be visible; or if you wear all white clothes, even a tiny spot of grease will show. If you smoke three packs of cigarettes a day and your lungs are filled with nicotine, smoking a cigarette, or even a whole pack, is nothing to you. But after you have practiced Yogic breathing for a few weeks or months and have eliminated the nicotine from your lungs, if you get even a small whiff of cigarette smoke, you will feel as if you are suffocating.

It is the same with Yogic diet. A clean body will notice even a little heavy or unclean food and will be affected by it. But that is only until it becomes completely clean and strong. After a certain stage, you can even eat anything you want and not be affected. A young plant needs a fence around it until it grows into a tree. Once it is fully grown, not only does it not need the fence, but it can give shade to the other plants and to animals. Be gentle with your body until it really becomes strong. You may think, "I have been so good this whole week, now I deserve to celebrate a little and have some ice cream and cake;" but you should know that what is a celebration to you might well be a torture for your body.

It may inspire you to hear of a spiritual vow that many people take in India. I am not talking about the monks now, but about the simple village people. Lord Vishnu is said to use a golden eagle named Garuda for a vehicle. Therefore, whenever his devotees see a golden eagle, they are reminded of him. Many of them take a vow called "Seeing the Golden Eagle." This means they will not eat on that day until or unless they see a golden eagle. On some days they might not see one until three or four o'clock in the afternoon. Other days they might not see one at all; on those days they do not take any food. I have met people who have kept this vow for thirty or forty years. That is control over the tongue.

Conclusion

We learn many things from the animals and birds. They eat simple, natural food and never have to go to the doctor. They never need pills for constipation or insomnia, or to get rid of gas. It is because they live according to nature. Mahatma Gandhi used to say very often, "Go back to nature. You will enjoy everything that is good in life." Our society has become unnatural in so many respects: our food is artificial, our dress is artificial, even so much of our thinking has become artificial. That is why we have so many problems - personal, interpersonal, national, international.

The aim of Yoga is to go back to nature as much as possible. To lead a natural life, with simple food, simple dress, simple living. Then naturally, the mind also will have "high" thinking. Once we start living simply, we will have the time to think high and to easily solve all our personal and world problems. Let there be a limitation in everything, a tranquility in everything. As the *Bhagavad Gita* says, "Yoga is not for the person who eats too much, nor for the one who fasts excessively." Going to extremes can sometimes be easier, but the middle path is what we need for a life of health and peace. Let us think in a peaceful way; eat in a peaceful way. Let all of our actions be done in this spirit. Let us be easeful, peaceful and useful.

Part III:
Getting Started

Balanced Diet, Balanced Life

by *Sandra McLanahan, M.D.*
Medical Director, Integral Health Services
Director of Stress Management Training
for the Preventive Medicine Research Institute

HOW TO EAT WELL AS A VEGETARIAN

Good health is not automatically guaranteed just because you are a vegetarian. No doubt, becoming a vegetarian is a step in the right direction; but one of the most important and central principles for good health is moderation—in diet and in your attitude in life.

A balanced diet means not taking anything to the extreme. Even the best ingredients in a diet may not make you healthy if you don't eat in a conscious, moderate and relaxed way.

WHAT NOT TO EAT

Four major medical studies have now shown that if serum cholesterol is lowered by dietary changes, the incidence of heart disease goes down. It is possible to prevent heart attacks by following a changed diet. Regression and reversal can also be attained.

In populations that follow a vegetarian diet the heart attack rate remains low, even when there is severe stress, such as war. Our health does best if we eat a vegetarian diet. If we put fats into our long intestinal tract, the body absorbs too much fat, and by the time we are eleven or twelve years old our arteries are streaked with fat. In addition, fats slow down the transit time of food through the bowels, again increasing the time these materials are in contact with the bowel wall. Fats in the diet may also affect the balance of hormones in our bodies. A high-fat, low-fiber diet has been linked to appendicitis, diverticulitis, colitis, osteoporosis, cataracts, arthritis, heart disease, strokes, diabetes, and cancers of the breast, uterus, prostate, ovary, colon and rectum.

59

Fats in the diet may call forth an increase in bile salts, digestive agents which are known to be cancer-causing substances. Meat diets are much higher in saturated fat—a type of fat more resistant to processing by the body and therefore more likely to clog the arteries. Cancer of the colon may be directly linked to the amount of saturated fat in the diet. Populations that eat such diets—especially diets high in beef—have a more elevated incidence of this cancer.

Plant sterols—complex hormone-like plant proteins—lower levels of cholesterol in the blood. Heart disease caused by elevated levels of blood cholesterol is responsible for one out of every two deaths in America.

WHEN TO EAT

It would be ideal if our appetites could be our guides. Unfortunately, our often overly-sedentary lives do not allow us to take in all that we would like to without ill effects.

It is best to ingest most of the calories in the earlier part of the day. Research has concluded that calories consumed earlier in the day cause less weight gain than the same amount eaten later in the day. The process of digestion slows down significantly as the day progresses, and even more dramatically during sleep.

Sri Swami Satchidananda's recommendations for a daily meal plan that consists of a light breakfast, main meal for lunch and light dinner, make the most sense to me. After a period of seven hours or more of "fasting" during the night, it is a good idea to "break-fast," as Sri Swamiji says, with just a beverage or fruits. For some people who are doing heavy physical labor, this may not be advisable, but for those following a more sedentary life, it seems highly favorable. The noon meal is the best time for the largest caloric intake of the day, with plenty of time in the remaining day, to digest and burn off the calories. Supper should be early as digestion greatly slows down at night, especially during sleep.

In one study, persons of normal weight were placed in a room with obese persons, and the clock on the wall was sped up. When the clock showed 12:00 noon—although in reality it was only 10:30 A.M., the overweight people took out their lunches and began to eat. Those who were at a more correct weight did not eat. We should not let the time of day rule our eating habits, but instead let our bodies and real appetite be our guide.

WHAT TO EAT

We've determined that vegetarian foods are the optimal foods for human beings to digest and assimilate. But it is not enough to say that by abstaining from meat, fish or eggs, one will be a healthy vegetarian.

The most simple and clear way to decide what is useful, from all the nutritional advice that abounds for vegetarians or even non-vegetarians, is to use the principle: "Eat what is natural." This means to eat, as much as possible, foods as they occur in nature. "Organically Grown," "Whole Foods," "No Preservatives," "No Additives" are all labels that describe natural foods.

Foods can be prepared in a way that preserves their natural state as much as possible. Fruits are best taken raw. Vegetables can be taken raw or lightly steamed. If we eat an apple, our blood sugar stays at a nice and steady level. If we eat apple sauce, the blood sugar rises, then falls.

Pectin is higher in a vegetarian diet. Pectin is a complex carbo-hydrate found in many fruits. One study showed a 5% drop in cholesterol in just three weeks when 15 grams (the usual vegetarian diet level) was given daily. Apples are high in pectin. An apple a day may very well keep the doctor away!

Whole foods are unprocessed foods. When rice is refined, the bran and germ are taken out and all nutrients and fibers are lost. Whole grains are an essential part of the human diet. Removal of fiber from goods by processing—as is done with white flour or white rice—has been implicated in the development of appendi-citis, diverticulosis and diverticulitis, colitis, hemorrhoids, varicose veins, gall stones, cancer of the colon and diabetes. There is now a vast amount of evidence to support the thesis that natural food prevents a wide variety of illnesses.

Dr. Denis Burkitt has called the United States "the most con-stipated country in the world." A high fiber, vegetarian diet can provide the daily bowel movement that avoids sludging in the bowel. That regularity is thought to reduce colon cancer.

Fiber is that portion of the food that passes through the digestive tract without being absorbed. Fiber in the diet has many protective properties. It decreases the amount of carbohydrate that we absorb from our food and probably assists in protection from diabetes and allows diabetes to be treated more effectively once present. Fiber in the diet increases the amount of fat that passes through and out the digestive system, decreasing the amount of fat that is actually absorbed and thus may block the arteries. Increased fiber has been found to lower the level of low-density cholesterol—the "bad" cholesterol associated with fatty buildup in the arteries.

Returning to a whole, natural, vegetarian diet can be a surprising delight. The result is an easefulness of the bowels and corresponding ease of other body functions.

HOW MUCH TO EAT

Animal studies have shown doubled and tripled lifespans in groups fed a low-calorie diet. The diseases of aging and disturbed immunity were avoided: diabetes, cardiovascular deterioration, renal disease, cancer. Overweight human females have 8-10 times the rate of cancers of the uterus and breast. About two-thirds of Americans are overweight. About one-third are enough above their ideal weight to cause serious disease such as high blood pressure, diabetes, and gall bladder diseases with attendant chronic disability and shortened life expectancy.

The excess consumption of fats and refined foods, may impair our immune status. In one study, persons fed a high protein diet had an increase in malaria, tuberculosis and brucellosis.

On the other hand, fixation upon diet and weight can lead to so much stress in the mind, it may manifest as a disease itself. With consideration to constitutional factors, an ideal weight cannot merely be taken from a table, but is best formulated by a combination of risk factors, psychological and social aspects, and medical assessment, forming a holistic view.

One of the worst problems, of course, is knowing just how much to eat or even how to stop eating once we've begun. This is a matter of discipline and awareness that can be cultivated by practice. Techniques such as using a small plate or bowl and taking just the right amount of food, then washing the dish immediately after eating and moving onto a pleasant activity, may help keep the mind from temptations to overeat.

Becoming more in tune with our bodies and developing will-power so we are the masters instead of the slaves to our own desires are very desirable goals. I generally recommend yoga practice for those people who want to develop this kind of inner strength. What is particularly unique about yoga practice is its ability to offer a good overall approach to preventive medicine. The basic program trains the body and mind to be at your control and to be able to replace harmful habits with positive actions and attitudes. Once established in this lifestyle, one automatically becomes a healthy vegetarian.

HOW TO EAT

It is not just the type of food or the quantity of food, but the attitude and lack of stress with which we take our food that determines its ultimate effect.

To facilitate greater awareness of how and why we eat, it may be useful to keep a "Diet Awareness Chart." List the date, time, location and mood you are in whenever you eat something. This will heighten your consciousness and may help you to have more control in determining when and how you will eat.

When you eat, it's an important practice in increasing your awareness and in aiding digestion, to slow down. "Chew liquids and liquify solids" is an ancient adage that is full of practical wisdom. It may help to make a determined effort to find a quiet spot where you can concentrate on eating and not engage in conversation. It has been shown by some ingenious laboratory experiments that the body works best if it can focus its blood supply at the digestive tract after food is put there.

Remember that the main function of eating is to preserve the strength of the physical form in order for us to maintain a healthy lifestyle.

WHEN NOT TO EAT

The unending, sometimes strange, stream of food materials

thrust on the digestive system to sort out and assimilate, is often consumed without much reflection upon its effect on the magnificent instrument the human body.

One aim in following a healthy vegetarian diet is to increase our consciousness of our bodies and what we put into them. We need to avoid overloading the digestive tract, and allow it time for revitalization and any needed repairs. It can't focus upon repairs if it must continue to process foods. That is why it's most important to take greater care in regard to food intake and types of foods when the body is in a weakened or overtired condition.

Abstaining from food was originally called "fasting" from the word "fast," meaning to hold firm to something. The word may also have derived from the observation that it helped make the individual healthy quickly.

Fasting is a very useful, natural technique for relieving many physical and even mental problems. A cautious approach is recommended however. The body generally works better when changes are made gradually. You can ensure easeful fasting by following certain recommendations which follow.

Fasting is a simple, ancient remedy not often used in the West. We sometimes hear the saying "Feed a cold, starve a fever." The adage has lost its original intent through the years. The saying began, "If you feed a cold, then you'll have to starve a fever." It was intended to convey that if you eat while having a cold, you may then become so sick with fever that you'll have to fast to get rid of the illness.

Animals naturally fast when they are ill. Did you ever notice that it is difficult to try and force them to eat? Children are also often this way. Why is this so? Fasting gives the body, especially the digestive tract, a chance to rest from expending the energy required to digest and assimilate food. The stomach, intestines, liver and pancreas are constantly working on the food we eat. During a fast, they have time to rest and repair. That means the body is able to send more of its blood supply to weak areas.

Almost all diseases can be benefited by moderate fasting, including arthritis, arteriosclerosis and resulting high blood pressure, and infections. Of course, the word "moderation" again comes into play and we must realize that our bodies need food in order to function well. Moderate fasting allows desirable blood shift effects without detriment. Laboratory studies have proven that fewer infections and degenerative processes occur when fasting every few days is incorporated into laboratory animals' routines.

Other times when it's perhaps not a good idea to eat are when you're very upset or too rushed or feeling stressed. Many studies have documented that digestive enzymes are not adequately secreted when emotions are high. Food can literally just sit in your stomach or intestines and ferment as if turning to poison.

Probably if we always ate just the right foods, in just the right amounts and with the right attitude, there would be little need to fast.

ABOUT INTEGRAL HEALTH SERVICES

The first Integral Health Services (IHS) was established in 1976 in Putnam, Connecticut, as a cooperative holistic health care practice. According to the IHS philosophy, health is not merely the absence of disease. A healthy person is someone who has all aspects of life balanced and integrated. A healthy person is conscious of how the physical, nutritional, emotional, environmental and spiritual aspects of life affect health.

Prevention magazine featured IHS as a pioneer in its approach: combining western and eastern medicine, chiropractic, nutrition counseling, therapeutic massage, psychological counseling, and yoga therapy.

In 1980, while the first IHS continued to serve in Connecticut, a second IHS was established in Buckingham, Virginia. It currently sponsors health retreats and is planning other programs with an eye toward establishing a complete residential health retreat center.

For more information please write: Integral Health Services, Route 1, Box 180D, Buckingham, VA. 23921. Telephone: (804) 969-4680

THE PREVENTIVE MEDICINE RESEARCH INSTITUTE

The Institute was established by Dr. Dean Ornish, whose work in the field of preventive medicine, specifically in relation to heart disease, has been recognized world-wide.

"Stress, Diet and Your Heart" is Dr. Ornish's best-selling book based on the scientific research and studies he conducted at the Baylor College of Medicine. Both Sri Swami Satchidananda and Dr. Sandra McLanahan collaborated on this work.

Now, Dr. Ornish supervises residential and out-patient programs, through the Institute, to help patients heal heart disease through stress reduction techniques and dietary changes without additional drugs or surgery.

Dr. Ornish is also a member of the Board of Integral Health Services.

For more information on PMRI write: PMRI, 2302 Divisadero Street, San Francisco, CA 94115

Helpful Hints for New Vegetarians

by Swami Premananda Ma

If you are a new vegetarian, we would like to offer some basic and informative guidelines and instructions to assist you in your transition from a non-vegetarian diet to a vegetarian, whole foods diet.

Here are a seven-day "starter" meal plan and recipes. Feel free to adapt and adjust the menu to suit your needs. You will probably be familiar with most of the ingredients listed; but, just in case, we are listing some that may be new to you along with information on cooking certain foods, sprouting, using a wok, etc. To make your transition smoother, you may wish to first eliminate red meats and eat only chicken and fish. Then stop eating chicken. Next, you can leave seafood behind; and finally eliminate eggs from your diet.

There are a number of companies that are now producing "imitation meat" products or ready-made foods that are perfect substitutes for those items you thought you'd never be able to live without such as:

Non-Vegetarian	Vegetarian Alternative
sausage	soy links
bacon	soy strips
luncheon meats	tofu or tempeh in slices that are so similar in consistency, shape, flavor and packaging to bologna, salami, etc.

egg salad .... tofu spreads

hamburgers ..... soy, nut and tempeh burgers either in mixes or frozen

chicken .... tofu sliced, wrapped in cellophane and frozen. Later, defrost the tofu by letting it sit in a bowl of boiling water for 20-30 minutes. It tastes like and has the consistency of pieces of chicken.

And if you're trying to cut down on dairy, fats and cholesterol:

Dairy	Non-dairy Alternative
cheese	soyarella cheese that melts like mozzarella
ice cream	tofu, soy or rice "ice creams" that look and taste like the real thing
milk	soy milk (plain or flavored— malted is very nice)
butter	soy margarine
ricotta cheese ...	tofu adapts as a perfect substitute in fillings for lasagne and casseroles
cream cheese	tofu blended until creamy works beautifully for cheesecake and other dessert recipes

We highly recommend a trip to your local natural/health food store. It will be fun and also greatly informative. Usually the store manager or staff members can answer your questions or point you in the right direction to get the information you need.

Partial Listing of Some Basic Ingredients

GRAINS

BROWN RICE is high in fiber and vitamins as well as minerals. It is mainly available in long or short grain. Rinse well in cold water. Cook 1 c. rice to 3 c. water. Bring water to boil, add rice and boil for 3 minutes. Then reduce the heat and simmer covered for 45 minutes.

MILLET is a very wholesome whole grain—yellow in color, high in B-complex vitamins and protein. It is rich in minerals including calcium and iron. Use 2 parts water to 1 part grain. Bring to a boil and then let simmer, covered, for 40 minutes. Slightly nutty flavor. A good rice substitute.

COUS-COUS is best known for its use in Middle Eastern dishes. It is a cracked wheat, that has usually been pre-cooked and then dehydrated; that is why it cooks so quickly. You can boil water (1 c. cous-cous to 1 c. water), add the cous-cous—plus a pat of butter if desired—and then turn off the heat. Let pot sit covered for 5—10 minutes. Or if you want it to be softer, you can use 1 c. cous-cous to 2 cups water. Let it boil for 3 minutes; then reduce the heat to a simmer for about 5-7 minutes more. Turn off the heat and let it finish cooking for another 5-7 minutes.

FLOUR

WHOLE WHEAT. Made from wheat berries, this type of flour generally retains most of the bran and wheat germ. Stone ground flour is the best because more of the nutrients are retained when it is processed this way.

WHOLE WHEAT PASTRY FLOUR is made from soft wheat berries. It has less gluten than whole wheat flour. That is why pastry flour is used mainly for baking.

SOY FLOUR is made from whole soybeans. This is a gluten-free flour and is popular with people on gluten-free diets. If you are trying to reduce gluten intake, it may be used in combination with whole wheat flour.

WHEAT GERM. The wheat berry's center is known as the "germ." It is high in B-complex vitamins and vitamin E as well as many important minerals. Though one often sees toasted wheat germ in the supermarket, it is preferable to use it raw, as toasting destroys some of the vitamins and minerals.

BRAN. The wheat berry's outer layer is what is known as "bran." High in dietary fiber and B-complex vitamins and trace minerals.

LEGUMES

Dried beans and peas are wonderfully versatile. Add to soups or add vegetables to them and serve with rice. Basic cooking instructions: 1 cup of legumes to 3 or 4 cups of water. One cup of legumes will yield about 2½ cups when cooked. A staple in many of the Eastern countries, legumes often take the place of meat. They are a good source of protein, iron and B-complex vitamins without the cholesterol and fat of meat. (As you rinse legumes before cooking, be sure to check for little stones. There are often a few that have been missed in the commercial cleaning process, but you will easily see them. The extra time is worth it. Encountering one while chewing is not a pleasant experience!)

LENTILS cook easily in 45 minutes to 1 hour and are a good source of protein. (see East Indian section for further information on legumes such as "dhals")

SOY PRODUCTS

TOFU is made from soybeans, water and a solidifier. It is also known as "bean curd" or "soy cheese." It is high in protein and calcium. Tofu comes packaged in water to preserve its freshness. It keeps well for one week if you're diligent about rinsing and changing the water daily. Needs to be refrigerated.

TEMPEH is a culture of either just cooked soybeans or cooked soybeans in combination with grains such as rice or wheat. Available at health food stores, it is high in protein, B12 and other B-complex vitamins.

OILS

SAFFLOWER and CORN OIL are the oils high in polyunsaturates (which help to reduce serum cholesterol).

OLIVE OIL and SESAME OIL are excellent for your health.

SEASONINGS

TAMARI (or "shoyu"). This is a soy sauce that is more naturally fermented than others. Also, it has no additives.

TAHINI is ground sesame seed paste which is high in protein and delicious added to dressings, dips and spreads. It's great for kids when mixed with honey and spread on bread or crackers!

SEA SALT is recommended instead of table salt because it is less refined and is processed without chemicals.

VEGETABLE SALTS. There is an incredible range of salts that are mixed with various herbs. Some of the most popular are called: "Spike," "Vegit," "Lemon Pepper," "Herbamare."

UNSALTED SEASONINGS. There is a complete range of unsalted seasonings that combine various herbs and are often categorized by cuisine including Italian, Mexican, Chinese, and also Garlic with Herbs. There are exotic blends such as "Nile Spice" which combines cumin, coriander, sesame seeds and more. "Cleopatra's Secret" contains sesame seeds, garlic, chili powder, cayenne, cumin and more.

Even if you take salt, one secret to varying your preparation of dishes is the combination of spices you use. With "no-salt" seasonings you can combine as many varieties as you want to achieve unique flavors and then add the amount of salt you wish.

INDIAN SEASONINGS & SPICES

Enjoy a walk through an Indian grocery store. The smells coming from the spice section are entrancing! Exotic as they seem, the spices and ingredients used in Indian cooking are very simple and delightful once you learn a bit about them. Several of the seasonings you will find in the recipes listed in this book are:

TURMERIC (haldi). Bright yellow in color, it gives color (though not much flavor) to various dishes and is known in India for its profound medicinal properties. In ancient times, women cleansed their skin with this root of a plant that is sold in powdered form. It is believed to be a blood purifier and general body toner.

BLACK MUSTARD SEED. This little black seed has its counterpart in the yellow mustard seed used in the West. These seeds are basic to most recipes and provide a subtle flavor.

SAFFRON. Gorgeously fragrant and expensive, this spice comes from a crocus flower of Kashmir and Spain. Gives a beautiful orangey color to rice dishes and Indian sweets.

GARAM MASALA is very popular in North Indian dishes, this is a beautifully aromatic, ready-made, powdered combination of a number of spices, including cloves, cinnamon, nutmeg, cardamom and black pepper.

INDIAN GRAINS & LEGUMES

SPLIT MOONG DHAL has a light yellow color. This, of all the varieties of Indian *dhal* or lentils, is the most nutritious and very easy to prepare. Clean the *dhal* well and bring twice the amount of water to boil. Add the *dhal* and boil gently for about 35 minutes until soft.

MASOOR DHAL. Reddish-orange in color, this is the quickest cooking *dhal*. Boil twice the amount of water and let gently boil for about 20 minutes.

BASMATI RICE is a very fragrant, long grain white rice that is not as completely refined as Western white rices. From North India and Pakistan. Perfect for special rice dishes. boil twice the amount of water and then add the cleaned and rinsed rice. Let boil for 3 minutes; then cover and simmer for 20 minutes.

SEA VEGETABLES

Sea vegetables are wonderful and versatile and are high in trace minerals, fiber and vitamins. There are usually basic cooking instructions on the packages. Varieties include:

NORI is perfect for making vegetarian *sushi*.

HIZIKI is good to add to salads, soups or vegetable dishes.

DULSE. Good sprinkled on salads and soups, it is also very versatile in its powdered form.

KELP. In powdered form, it is highly recommended to sprinkle on your foods as a good salt substitute.

WAKAME is very nice in vegetable or bean dishes or in soups.

KOMBU makes wonderful, nutritious soup stock. It's also good in bean dishes.

SPROUTS

Sprouts are often considered the best source of raw food nutrition. They have an easily digestible form and contain iron, calcium, protein, and vitamins B and C.

You can buy sprouts ready-to-eat, but it's healthier and more fun to grow them yourself. While there are many sprouting kits for sale, you can easily put one together using a Ball jar (or any wide-mouth glass jar) and a piece of cheesecloth. Sprouts are delicious, great in salads and sandwiches. You can buy the seeds at your health food store. Among the seeds and legumes great for sprouting: alfalfa, radish, green lentils, chick peas, and mung beans.

Place about 2 Tbs. of seeds in a quart-sized jar and cover the jar with the cheesecloth (or a fine mesh screen). Use a rubber band (or if you use a Ball jar, screw on the open ring only to hold the cloth in place. Rinse the seeds well and then soak them in the jar by filling it with about 8 oz. of water. Let them sit overnight (about 8-10 hours). Drain the water, rinse the seeds with lukewarm water, and drain them again. Rinse several times until the water is clear. Then let the seeds continue to drain by resting the jar, at a slant, with the mouth downward. Rinse and drain the seeds several times a day and keep them in a warm place out of direct sunlight. After they reach the desired length, you can then put them in the sun and they will absorb the light and being to turn green (chlorophyll is released). Keep them in the refrigerator and use within a week.

SPECIAL ITEMS

EGG REPLACER. All our recipes are eggless. "Jolly Joan" or other egg replacers work wonderfully well. Get this powder in your health food store.

ESSENE BREAD. This is a "bread" made from sprouted grains alone. It is easier to digest than regular wheat flour breads because it is sprouted.

NUT MILK. For those who wish to avoid dairy products, nut milks provide a very pleasing alternative. Nowadays you can easily find soy milk, unflavored or in a variety of tasty flavors, in any health food store; or you can easily make your own.

Healthful Methods of Cooking

STEAMING

Steaming your vegetables and tofu is one of the easiest and most healthful ways of cooking. Valuable minerals are not lost, as happens with boiling or overcooking. A stainless steel vegetable steamer can be purchased in almost any store and will probably fit into one of your cooking pots. Place the steamer in the pot and add water to a level just below the bottom of the basket. Steam to the desired tenderness. You can also make use of the remaining water in the pot, by using it when you cook, adding it to soups etc.!

WOK COOKING

Wok cooking is also a wonderful way to prepare vegetables especially if you wish to saute them, bringing out the flavor using oil or butter. Woks are made from various metals and we recommend the rolled steel, non-electric type.

After you purchase a wok, you must clean it well. Wash and scrub it with an abrasive cleanser to remove the machine oil. Then place it on its ring, over your burner. Fill the wok with water and boil for a couple of hours. It's a good idea to keep the water level up to the very brim of the wok so that a water ring isn't left as it boils. Pour out the water and, if you wish, you can repeat the process a second time. After this, dry the wok by placing it on the burner over heat. When it's dry, rub vegetable oil into the wok using paper towels. You may notice a black residue when you wipe the wok with the paper towel. This is the protective coating it comes with and you should continue to wipe the wok with oil until there is no more visible residue.

After each use, it's important to clean your wok with a wok brush or sponge in sudsy water. Do not use abrasives now, because you are building a well-seasoned wok. It's sufficient to clean it with the sudsy water and then dry over high heat and then rub it lightly with a teaspoon or so of oil. Then store the wok.

MEAL PRAYER

Before each meal at Satchidananda Ashram, the following prayer is recited. The prayer is in the ancient Sanskrit language, renowned for its profound and calming vibrational qualities. By offering a prayer before meals, we are reminded of several things: We eat to live (rather than living to eat). We have gratitude for the many blessings in our lives. We take a few moments to calm the mind and prepare the body to receive nourishment.

OM Annapoorne Sadaapoorne*
Sankara Praana Vallabhe
Jnaana Vairaagya Siddhyartham
Bhikshaam Deehee cha Paarvati
Maataa cha Paarvathi Devee
Pitaa Devo Maheswaraha
Baandhavaah Siva Bhaktaaha
Swadeso Bhuvana Tryam
Hari Om Tat Sat Brahmaarpanamastu
Lokaah Samastaah Sukhino Bhavantu

OM Beloved Mother Nature,
You are here on our table as our food.
You are endlessly bountiful, benefactress of all.
Please grant us health and strength, wisdom and dispassion
    to find permanent peace and joy.
Mother Nature is my mother,
My father is the Lord of all.
All the peoples are my relatives,
The entire universe is my home.
I offer this unto OM,
That Truth which is Universal.
May the entire creation be filled with peace and joy, love and light.

*S = the sound of "s" in "sure" or "show"

Seven Day Vegetarian Menu Plan

MONDAY ——————————

Breakfast .... Brown Rice Cream with
Nut Milk
Fresh Fruits

Lunch .... Mediterranean Delight
Veggie Casserole

Supper .... Hearty Vegetable Soup
Toast or Crackers

TUESDAY ——————————

Breakfast .... Granola with
Nut Milk
Fresh Fruits

Lunch .... Brown Rice
Tofu
Steamed Vegetables

Supper .... Fruit Soup

WEDNESDAY ——————————

Breakfast .... Fresh Fruit Cup
Toast or Muffins

Lunch .... Vegetable Salad with
Salad Dressing
Guacamole with Chips
or Toast

Supper .... Veggie Melt
Whole Wheat Toast

THURSDAY

Breakfast .... Fruit Smoothee

Lunch .... Un-Hamburger with
                      Whole Wheat Bun
                      Steamed Vegetables
                      Potato Salad

Supper .... Spiced Cream of
                      Wheat *(Uppuma)*
                      Yogurt

FRIDAY

Breakfast .... Raisin and Bran Muffins
                      Jam or Apple Butter
                      Apple Juice

Lunch .... Chinese Feast of:
                      Fried Rice
                      Mixed Chinese Vegetables
                      Chinese Bean Curd

Supper .... Tofu Salad Sandwich

SATURDAY

Breakfast .... Scrambled Tofu
                      Toast
                      Orange juice

Lunch .... East Indian Feast of
                      Pilau Rice
                      Curried Vegetables
                      Spiced Dhal

Supper .... Rainbow Pasta Salad

SUNDAY

Breakfast .... Whole-Grain Pancakes
Fresh Fruits

Lunch .... Vegetarian Lasagne
Garlic Bread

Supper .... Premala's Angel Cream

ABBREVIATIONS *(in recipes)*

---

c. = cup
tsp. = teaspoon
Tbsp. = tablespoon
oz. = ounce
lb. = pound

FOR INFORMATION ON VEGETARIAN COOKING CLASSES:

Contact: Satchidananda Ashram—Yogaville,
Buckingham, VA 23921
or your nearest Integral Yoga Institute

Breakfast Recipes

Brown Rice Cream

This is a wonderful whole-grain (i.e. high fiber) alternative to the refined Cream of Wheat or Cream of Rice cereals. Erewhon and several other natural food companies make a very easy to prepare Brown Rice Cream cereal which takes only about 3 minutes to cook. If you'd like to prepare this cereal from scratch you'll be surprised to find it almost as simple as "store-bought."

¾ c. brown rice, uncooked
4 c. of low-fat milk, water
  (or nut milk)
l tsp. salt (optional)

Wash the rice and drain the water. Place the rice in a pan (no oil) and roast it. Keep stirring, and after about 5 minutes or so you will begin to smell the fragrance of the rice. Continue to dry roast until the rice turns golden brown.

When roasted, let it cool down and then place the rice in the blender and blend it until it is fine (i.e. fine semolina consistency). Then roast it again in a dry pan. Let it cool. (Note: you can prepare the rice this way in quantities for future use as long as you store it in a tightly covered jar.)

Heat the milk and bring it to the boiling point. As soon as the milk boils, if desired you can add the salt and then lower the heat and let the milk simmer for about 10 minutes. Now, slowly add the ground rice as you keep stirring. Within 3-5 minutes the rice cream should come to a desirable thickness.

Yield: Four servings.

Delightful to serve with raisins, bananas, honey and a dash of cinnamon.

Cashew Milk

A very simple and flavorful nut milk to prepare is Cashew Milk. We find nut milks wonderful for adding to cereals, in preparing gravies and for use in making smoothies.

1 c. raw cashews
1 quart of water
1 Tbs. soy or safflower oil
2 Tbs. honey
¼ tsp. salt (optional)

Place all the ingredients in the blender until well blended and the mixture becomes milk-like. If you refrigerate the cashew milk, it will be even tastier.

Whole cashews tend to be very expensive these days so we recommend using cashew pieces which are sold at health food stores for about half the price.

Granola

Another very popular breakfast cereal that's packed with high energy and fiber is granola. It's also readily available in health food stores and even in many supermarkets. It is quite easily prepared at home and can be stored in a tightly closed container or in the fridge for weeks. The aroma and flavor of home-baked granola is divine!

3 c. rolled oats
1 c. raw or toasted
  wheat germ
⅛-¼ c. sesame seeds
⅛-¼ c. sunflower seeds
½ c. raisins or sultanas
¼ c. soy or safflower oil
½ tsp. vanilla extract
¼ c. honey (Clover honey
  has a light taste and is
  especially good for this
  recipe.)
½-1 tsp. nutmeg
½-1 tsp. powdered
  cinnamon

Pre-heat your oven to 300 degrees F.

Place all the dry ingredients, except the raisins, in a mixing bowl and mix together. On a low flame, heat the honey, oil and vanilla. When warm, pour it over the dry ingredients, making sure the mixture gets well-coated, without lumps. Then spread the mixture out in a large, shallow baking pan and bake for about 35-45 minutes, until lightly browned. It's important to stir the mixture every 10 minutes so it will bake evenly and the edges don't burn. Or bake in a slow oven (200 degrees) for 2 hours. Add the raisins for the last 10 minutes of baking. Let cool.

Other enjoyable variations or additions include: shredded coconut, chopped dates or figs, chopped nuts.

Yield: 2 quarts

Fruit Smoothee

With a little creativity and imagination you can make this into a quick morning beverage, a full breakfast or a dessert-like treat. The very adaptable fruit smoothee takes on a variety of guises and applications depending on what mood you're in.

Version #1:

½ c. fresh strawberries or peaches
2 c. low-fat milk, nut milk or water
2 ice cubes
Honey or maple syrup (if desired)

Mix ingredients in the blender, and you have a fast and deliciously filling—yet easily digestible—breakfast drink.

Version #2:

Follow Version #1 but substitute frozen strawberries or 1 frozen banana (or both) and you've got a Frozen Milkshake.

Version #3:

Follow Version #2 but add in a scoop of your favorite ice cream or soy ice cream and malted milk or malted soy milk and you've got a Frozen Thickshake.

Version #4:

½ c. low-fat yogurt
½ c. soy milk or apple juice
1 banana
2 Tbs. wheat germ (and bran)
2 Tbs. protein powder
Honey or other sweetener if desired

Mix these in the blender, and now you've got a real Healthshake.

Try your own varieties with other fresh fruit combinations.

Raisin and Bran Muffins

These muffins are a perfect breakfast treat. Nourishing and wholesome, they can be served with fresh fruit or packed for breakfast to go.

1 c. whole wheat flour
½ c. bran flakes
½ c. wheat germ
1 c. plain low-fat or non-fat
  yogurt
egg substitute for
  equivalent of 2 eggs
3 tsp. baking powder
¼-½ c. honey
3 Tbs. safflower oil
½ c. raisins or sultanas

Yield: 10-12 muffins

Pre-heat your oven to 375 degrees F.

Mix the dry ingredients (except raisins & egg substitute) in one bowl and the wet ingredients in a separate mixing bowl. Add the egg substitute to the wet ingredients and beat the mixture well (you can use an electric mixer or food processor). Pour this mixture into the bowl of dry ingredients and stir only enough to moisten them. Now fold in the raisins.

Oil your muffin tins and fill them two-thirds full. Bake about 20 minutes or until the muffins turn a golden color.

Scrambled Tofu

If you thought you'd never survive a diet that didn't include Sunday morning's scrambled eggs, you're in for a wonderful surprise! Versatile tofu is a welcome substitute for scrambled eggs — you'll love the flavor and you won't miss the cholesterol!

10 oz. tofu (soft tofu works
  better than firm for
  this recipe)
⅓ c. onion, thinly sliced
2 Tbs. safflower or
  sesame oil
½-1 tsp. herb seasoning
¼ tsp. turmeric
¼ tsp. salt
2 tsp. tamari

Yield: 2-3 servings

Heat the oil in a frying pan and saute the onions until soft. Add the seasonings and stir until they are well-mixed. Turmeric is usually available in supermarkets and also in Indian grocery stores, as this spice comes from India. Crumble the tofu and add to the frying pan. Saute until it is well-heated.

Variation: To make a more exotic version of this dish, you can add more Indian or Mexican seasonings such as ⅛ tsp. of ground cumin, ¼ tsp. ground coriander. For a spicier dish, add a dash of cayenne (ground red pepper) and dash of black pepper.

Whole-Grain Pancakes

For those in a hurry, whole-wheat instant mixes are a great substitute for the refined, white flour version. Mixes are available in any health food store; but here is an easy, homemade version:

1 c. whole wheat flour
⅓ c. soy flour -or-
  1-½ c. whole wheat flour
¼ c. corn flour
3 tsp. baking powder
2 c. milk (or ½ milk,
  ½ water)
Egg substitute for
  equivalent of 2 eggs
3 Tbs. safflower or soy oil
2 Tbs. honey or maple
  syrup

*Yield: approximately 20-24
  4-inch pancakes*

Mix together all the dry ingredients. In another bowl, mix all the liquid ingredients. Then pour the liquid into the dry ingredients and stir to a nice smooth batter consistency. (You can add more flour or more milk to adjust the consistency).

Lightly oil the skillet and heat. When very hot, pour some batter onto the skillet. After bubbles appear on the surface of the pancake, turn it over and let it turn golden brown on the second side.

Serve hot with any variety of toppings including fresh fruits, preserves, apple butter or good old-fashioned maple syrup.

Lunch Recipes

THE VEGETABLE CASSEROLE

This is one of our favorite and most versatile recipes. A casserole can be prepared the night before and heated when you want to serve it. It can be made with a variety of ingredients and makes a wonderful main course.

Mediterranean Delight

2 c. cous-cous
1 vegetable bouillon cube
2-3 medium-size beets, chopped
3 medium carrots, chopped
1 clove garlic, minced
½ small onion or scallions, chopped
¼ c. chopped black olives
½ tsp. chopped fresh ginger root
1 tsp. ground cumin
1 tsp. chopped parsley (fresh or dried)
½ tsp. dill
½ tsp. salt (optional)
dash of pepper
2-3 Tbsp. of olive or soy oil
½ c. of sesame gravy

Prepare the cous-cous. To do so, bring 4 cups of water to a boil and add the vegetable bouillon. When it dissolves, pour in the cous-cous. We find that it helps to let the cous-cous boil for several minutes in order to make it very soft and fluffy. Then turn the flame down and let it simmer for about 5 minutes covered. Check to see if the water is mostly absorbed. If not, let it simmer for another few minutes. If most of the water is absorbed, turn off the flame and keep it covered. Let it sit another 5-10 minutes, and it will continue to steam and finish cooking. Set aside.

In a pot, heat the oil and add the onion and garlic. Saute until golden and add the vegetables. Saute for a few minutes and then add the ginger and spices. Stir the vegetables until the spices are well-mixed. Cover the pot and let the vegetables cook to the desired consistency. You may need to add a little water. When the vegetables are done, take out a casserole dish and layer it with cous-cous and vegetables. First put ⅓ of the cous-cous and then ⅓ of the vegetables, ⅓ of the cous-cous and so on. Pour the gravy over the top (or if you prefer, place thinly-sliced muenster, mozzarella or other cheese on top) and bake for about 10 minutes at 300 degrees F.

Variations:

This basic casserole recipe can be adapted

to almost any vegetable and any combination of spices. Try other grains, substituting millet, rice or whole-wheat noodles (macaroni, spirals, or shells work well).

Another delicious and nutritious variation is to have one layer of tofu. Crumble 4 oz. of tofu and mix in the same seasonings listed in the recipe or "Spike" or any unsalted vegetable seasoning. Add as a layer to the casserole.

Yield: 4 servings.

Sesame Gravy

½ c. sesame tahini
¼ c. water
⅛ c. lemon juice
1 Tbs. chopped onion or
    scallion
¼ tsp. salt

Blend all the ingredients except the tahini in the blender. In a bowl mix the tahini and the blended ingredients together. Warm the gravy and use in the Vegetable Casserole or pour the gravy over rice (or other grain) and serve with vegetables.

Yield: 1 cup

Brown Rice   Tofu   Steamed Vegetables

This is a very basic menu that is served often for lunch at Satchidananda Ashram. You can vary your preparation of the tofu, add various seasonings to your rice and/or vegetables and have a different dish each day. Or just vary your vegetables and you have a simple, already planned menu for the week.

Baked Tofu

16 oz. of "firm style" tofu
2 thin slices of fresh
  ginger
1 clove garlic
1 Tbs. lemon juice
1 tsp. sesame oil
1 ½ oz. tamari
1 oz. water

Yield: 4 servings

Preheat oven to 350 degrees F.

Cut the tofu into ½ inch slices and place them flat in an unoiled baking dish. In the blender, mix the rest of the ingredients. Pour this mixture over the tofu and place uncovered in the oven. Bake 30 minutes.

Note: See section on preparing brown rice and steaming vegetables for the rest of this lunch's recipes.

Steamed Tofu

This method of preparing tofu allows it to really take on any flavoring you desire. It maximizes its ability to absorb and thus makes it so versatile.

Cut 16 oz. of firm-style tofu into small cubes and place the cubes in a vegetable steamer. Steam for about 30 minutes. Then place the tofu in a serving dish and pour Sesame Gravy or any of your favorite sauces over the tofu. Let it stand for about 5-10 minutes to fully absorb the sauce before serving.

Pan-Fried Tofu

More healthful than deep-frying tofu, and perhaps tastier than baking it, is the pan-fried method.

You can pan-fry tofu by cutting it as you did in the Baked Tofu recipe and placing it in a skillet that is heated with 1 Tbs. of safflower or sesame oil. Mix 2 tsp. of tamari with 1 tsp. of any herb seasoning and some garlic and/or onion powder. Pour this over the tofu and let it saute for a few minutes on each side. You can serve as is, or pour Sesame Gravy or other sauce over it.

SALADS

For those who prefer to eat raw foods, the kitchen staff at Satchidananda Ashram prepares beautiful salads each day, as an alternative to cooked food. Mixing cooked food and raw food is not advised, and that is why you will not find this mixture in this menu section.

For those who think of salad as something dull or as a few lettuce leaves tossed together, there's a pleasant surprise coming. Did you know that there are many more than 10 basic types of salad greens? Each has a particular texture and flavor that can add a special flair to any salad. Explore the produce section of your supermarket. Be adventurous and experiment with different types of raw vegetables. Soon you'll be coming up with new and exciting variations all your own.

Most everyone can put together a simple salad, so we've just given you some fancy ones. You can take it from there.

Vegetable Salad

1 head of Boston butter lettuce
1 head of Romaine lettuce
1 c. shredded purple cabbage
1 c. grated carrots
1 c. grated beets
2 cucumbers, sliced
2 tomatoes, chopped (or use whole cherry tomatoes)
1 avocado chopped
1-2 stalks of celery, diced
1 green pepper, diced
1 small onion, thinly sliced (or use whole "cocktail" onions)
large handful of alfalfa, mung and/or other sprouts
any of your favorite vegetables vegetables — raw, cut into small pieces such as cauliflower, zucchini etc.

Yield: 4 servings

Toss together all the ingredients and top with any of a number of garnishes. Some suggestions: toasted sesame seeds, croutons, toasted almonds, black or green olives (or try stuffed olives), etc.

SALAD DRESSINGS

There are as many varieties of salad dressings as there are salads. Here are a few to get your creativity rolling.

Thick and Creamy Dressing

½ c. Safflower or Soy
"Mayonnaise"
½ c. ketchup
2 oz. crumbled tofu
2 cloves garlic
1 Tbs. chopped onion
2 Tbs. honey
⅛ tsp. pepper
⅛ tsp. cumin powder
½ tsp. basil
½ tsp. oregano
½ tsp. salt or use 1 tsp. of
any vegetable salt like
Vegit, Spike, Herbamare,
etc.

Mix together all the ingredients in a food processor or blender. Then adjust the seasonings to your taste and add water for desired consistency.

Yield: 1 cup

Herb and Oil Dressing

1 c. All Blend Oil or
safflower oil
⅓ c. lemon juice
1 clove garlic
¼ tsp. basil
¼ tsp. oregano
⅛ tsp. rosemary
⅛ tsp. black pepper
1 Tbs. chopped fresh
parsley
salt or vegetable salt
to taste

Mix together all the ingredients in a blender. Then adjust the herbs and salt.

Yield: 1 ⅓ cups

Guacamole

2 medium sized avocados,
  mashed
2 cloves garlic
2 Tbs. chopped onion
1 Tbs. lemon juice
1 small tomato, peeled
1 tsp. tamari
1 tsp. vegetable salt

Yield: about 1 ½ cups

Combine the ingredients in a food processor until the mixture becomes the consistency of a smooth dip or spread. Spread this mixture on Essene bread or rice cakes. It makes a tasty dip for raw vegetables.

Variations:
A dash of ground cumin adds a real
  Mexican flair.
Add a dash of cayenne pepper or chili
  powder for a spicy dish.

Un-Hamburgers

2 c. cooked, mashed
  brown lentils
¼ c. ground sunflower
  seeds
2 Tbs. chopped onion
1 clove garlic
3 Tbs. grated carrots
1 tsp. basil
1 tsp. oregano
2 Tbs. chopped fresh
  parsley
⅛ tsp. black pepper
2 Tbs. tamari
salt to taste

Yield: Serves 4

Pre-heat oven to 350 degrees.
  Mix the ingredients together in a bowl. Check seasonings and salt and adjust if necessary. Form the mixture into patties and place them on an oiled baking sheet. Bake for about 20 minutes (until medium brown). Then turn the patties over and let them brown on the other side (about 15 minutes). Serve them on buns or you can serve the patties as an entree with steamed vegetables as the side dish.

Variations:
Make a "Cheeseburger" by melting a
  slice of sharp cheddar, swiss cheese or
  "soyarella" on top of the patty.

Potato Salad

4 medium potatoes
1 tomato, diced
3 Tbs. chopped green
  pepper
2 oz. minced onion
¼ c. crumbled 'soft style'
  tofu
½ cucumber fine chopped
1 Tbs. apple cider vinegar
⅓ c. safflower or soy
  mayonnaise
½ tsp. garlic powder or
  garlic salt
⅛ tsp. black pepper
⅛ tsp. dry mustard
salt to taste

Yield: 4 servings

Boil the potatoes until they are tender; then dice them.

In a bowl mix the rest of the ingredients, except the tofu and potatoes. When well-mixed, add the potatoes and tofu and mix well. Adjust salt and seasonings.

CHINESE FEAST

Chinese Bean Curd

1½-2 oz. tamari
1 oz. water
1 thin slice of fresh ginger
1 Tbs. chopped onion
1 clove garlic
1 tsp. sesame oil
16 oz. firm-style tofu

Yield: 4 servings

Mix together in the blender or whisk the ingredients (except the tofu). Use this sauce to pour over the tofu, which can be baked, pan-fried or steamed.

Fried Rice

Just when you thought that there was no such thing as vegetarian fried rice! And better still, this is a great recipe for leftover rice.

2 c. of cooked basmati or
   short-grain brown rice
Egg replacer for the
   equivalent of 2 eggs
1 oz. bamboo shoots
1 small onion, sliced thinly
   or use scallions
2 slices of fresh ginger
1 clove garlic
1 oz. abalone mushrooms
1 Tbs. butter
2 Tbs. sesame oil (Chinese
   sesame oil adds a
   special flavor)
2 oz. frozen peas
2 oz. frozen corn niblets
1 Tbs. tamari
⅛ tsp. black pepper
1 tsp. vegetable salt
¼ tsp. turmeric (for color)

Yield: *4 servings*

Heat the oil in a saucepan and saute the onions until they are soft. Then add the ginger and garlic and let it saute for 1 minute. Now add the vegetables; saute for a few minutes. Add the seasonings and continue to saute over medium heat until cooked. Add the cooked rice. When it's well-mixed with the vegetables and seasonings, add the egg substitute and let it get mixed in. Be careful not to stir the mixture too much, as this breaks up the rice grains and the dish will become mushy.

Variations:
Add any of your favorite or leftover
   vegetables.

Mixed Chinese Vegetables

2 scallions
1 head of finely cut
  Chinese cabbage
2 stalks of celery, finely
  sliced
½ green bell pepper,
  chopped fine
½ c. mung bean sprouts
1 head of broccoli cut
  into flowerets
1 c. frozen snow peas
2 oz. baby corn
2 cloves garlic
3 slices of fresh ginger
3 Tbs. arrowroot (mix
  with 2 Tbs. cold water)
  or use corn starch
Chinese sesame oil or
  other vegetable oil
  for sauteing
Tamari

Yield: 4 servings

Let the wok heat over medium-high heat. When it is hot, add just enough oil (about 2-3 Tbs.) to make a necklace around the wok. After the oil slides down around the sides of the wok you will have a small pool in the center of the wok. With this oil hot, immediately add the scallions, ginger and garlic and saute them for about 2 minutes.

You can use any variety of vegetables that you like. The rule in cooking them in the wok is to saute them by starting with the lightest and moving toward the darkest, adding the varieties one by one. This way you start the longer-cooking vegetables first, gradually adding those that require less cooking time.

Begin to add the vegetables, and let them saute until tender. Once they are all added, sprinkle in tamari sauce to taste. To help speed the cooking, you may wish to add a little water, allowing the vegetables to steam, covered, over medium heat.

Mix the arrowroot and water until smooth. Lower the heat and pour the arrowroot over the cooked vegetables. Stir the mixture until you have a translucent, slightly thickened sauce. If you like, add more tamari and sprinkle toasted sesame seeds over your delectable creation.

Pilau Rice

2 cups of Basmati rice
  or millet
4 cardamom pods
4 cloves
1 stick of cinnamon
pinch of saffron
1 tsp. salt
½ tsp. ghee or butter

Prepare rice by removing any stones and washing it well.

Bring 4 cups of water to a rapid boil. In the meantime remove the cardamom kernels by slightly tapping the shell in a mortar and pestle. Add the kernels (not the shells) and the rest of the spices, along with the salt and butter to the boiling water. Now add the rice, and let it boil for about 3 minutes. Then reduce the heat and let the rice simmer, covered, for about 20 minutes.

If you are using millet, bring 4¼ cups of water to boil and then add the spices as above. Stir in the millet and then simmer over low heat for about 35 minutes (millet should be almost dry and well-cooked).

Curried Veggies

3 carrots, cut into small
  pieces
2 small heads of
  cauliflower, cut into
  small flowerettes
1 c. frozen peas
2 c. frozen green beans
2 tsp. salt
1 tsp. garam masala
¼ tsp. turmeric powder
¼ tsp. curry powder (or
  less if you don't care
  for hot spices)
3 Tbs. chopped onion
2 thin slices of ginger
2 Tbs. safflower oil

Saute the onions in the oil. When they are soft, add the spices and ginger. Let this saute for 1 minute, and then add the vegetables. Stir them well and let them get well coated in the spices. Saute for about 5 minutes over a low flame. Add salt and a little water to help cook the vegetables more quickly; then cover. Stir occasionally and check often until they are cooked to the desired tenderness.

Spiced Dhal

2 cups of split moong dhal
1 tsp. garam masala or
   cumin powder
¼ tsp. curry powder (or
   less if desired)
½ tsp. powdered ginger (or
   use fresh ginger)
3 Tbs. chopped onion
1 Tbs. safflower oil
salt to taste

Remove any small stones from the dhal and rinse it well in cold water. Place it in a deep pot of 4 cups of boiling water. Let it gently boil (it tends to foam up when it first cooks so you must keep an eye on it). The dhal should cook until it is very soft and it breaks and becomes a little mushy when you stir it (about half an hour). You may have to add a little water occasionally so it can cook well and does not stick. Don't add too much water at a time, because when it is cooked it should have a thick soup consistency.

Saute the onions in the oil. When they are soft add the spices and let them saute on a low heat for 1 minute. Then add this mixture to the dhal and mix well, adding salt to taste.

Yield: The Indian feast serves 4-6

Vegetarian Lasagne

TOMATO SAUCE
(can be prepared beforehand)

8 oz. of tomato puree
1 tomato, cut small
1 small onion, chopped
2 Tbs. olive oil
1 bay leaf
2 cloves garlic
1 tsp. basil
1 tsp. oregano
1-2 Tbs. parsley
1 tsp. salt
½ tsp. black pepper
½ tsp. honey

In a saucepan, add the onion to the hot oil. Saute the onions until they are transparent. The secret to having onions tasty and sweet is to be sure they don't stick or burn. Keep stirring and, if needed, add a bit more oil or water.

Add crushed garlic (use a garlic press if available). Add to the pot and saute for a few minutes. Then add the tomato puree and the fresh tomato. Add the seasonings and bring the mixture to a simmer. Cover and let simmer for one hour. Remove the bay leaf before serving.

FILLING

16 oz. ricotta (or tofu blended to ricotta consistency)
3 Tbs. grated mozzarella cheese
1 tsp. salt
¼ tsp. nutmeg (wonderful to grate it fresh.)
¼ tsp. black pepper
Egg replacer to the equivalent of 2 eggs

Combine all the ingredients in a bowl and mix well.

NOODLES

12 whole-wheat lasagne noodles

Follow instructions for cooking the noodles, adding the noodles one by one to rapidly boiling water. Adding 1 Tbs. of oil after the noodles are all in the pot, helps prevent them from sticking. Cook them only until ½ - ¾ tender and then drain and rinse in cold water. Place the noodles so they are lying flat.

Pre-heat oven to 375 degrees.

LAYERING

1 lb. of shredded mozzarella and ½ cup grated fresh parmesan or romano cheese

Using a 9" x 3" baking pan, layer the lasagne as follows:

Cover the bottom of the pan with a thin layer of sauce. Place ⅓ of the noodles as the first layer. Using a spoon, put dollops of the filling on the first layer (use ½ the filling.) Cover this layer with ⅓ of the sauce. Then sprinkle ⅓ of the mozzarella on top; add another layer using ⅓ of the noodles. Put the rest of the filling on top of these noodles, and use another ⅓ of sauce to cover this layer. Sprinkle another ⅓ of the mozzarella on top of this. Add the last layer of noodles. Cover them with the remaining sauce; then add the remainder of the mozzarella. Sprinkle parmesan or romano cheese on top.

Bake the lasagne covered with foil for about 35 minutes and then for 10 more minutes with foil removed.

Serve lasagne with whole-wheat garlic bread and steamed green beans tossed in butter, salt and pepper.

Variations:
Add a layer of cooked spinach or broccoli.
Add chopped black olives to the filling.

Yield: 6-8 servings

Supper Recipes

SOUPS

Soups can be as simple or extravagant as you have time for. Here we include one soup that is a meal in itself and one that can be prepared in just 10 minutes. Discover the variety of soups in between and enjoy!

Hearty Vegetable Soup

2 large potatoes, diced
1 small onion, chopped
1 clove garlic
2 medium carrots, chopped
2 stalks celery, chopped
1 c. of chopped broccoli
½ green pepper, diced
2 medium green zucchini, chopped
2 Tbsp. safflower oil
2 vegetable bouillon cubes
½ tsp. oregano
½ tsp. thyme
1 Tbsp. chopped parsley
¼ tsp. black pepper
½ c. cooked rice, beans or pasta (optional)
salt to taste

Boil 4 cups of water and add the vegetable bouillon cubes. When the cubes have dissolved, add the diced potatoes. Cover and let cook at a gentle boil until the potatoes are soft. Let this cool down and then place the potatoes and their water in the blender. Blend until smooth.

In a heavy-bottomed pot, saute the onion and garlic in the oil until golden. Then add all the vegetables (except the potatoes) and let them saute for about 5 minutes. Add the blended potato broth to this.

Bring the soup to a boil and then reduce the heat, add the seasonings, cover and let simmer for 45 minutes—1 hour.

If you desire a *richer* soup, just before serving add 1 cup of warm milk and stir it into the soup. For a *thicker* soup, before serving, puree in the blender half the soup and then return it to the pot.

Variations:
Vary the vegetables you use.
Make it spicy by adding ground cumin and cayenne.

Yield: 4-5 servings

The Ten Minute Soup

12 oz. frozen peas
12 oz. water
1 vegetable bouillon cube
3 Tbsp. chopped onion
1 clove garlic (optional)
⅛ tsp. black pepper
¼ tsp. basil
¼ tsp. thyme
Salt or vegetable salt
  to taste
½ c. milk (optional)

Bring the water to a boil and dissolve the bouillon cube in it. Add the peas, onion and garlic and let cook until peas are soft. Pour this into the blender and blend for ½ minute. Then add seasonings and blend again until smooth.

Return the pureed peas to the pot. Add more water if you wish the soup to be thinner or you can add the milk if you wish to make this "Cream of Pea" soup. Let it heat through, but do not boil.

Yield: *about 3 ½ cups (more if you add the milk)*

Fruit Soup

Soups do not have to be made only from vegetables. Here's a refreshing summer "soup" idea.

1 c. peeled, diced apples
1 c. peeled, diced pears
1 c. sliced peaches
¼-½ c. raisins or sultanas
1 c. blueberries
1 banana, unpeeled
3 Tbsp. honey
2 c. low-fat or non-fat
  yogurt
1 tsp. cinnamon powder
¼ tsp. ground cloves
1 c. fruit juice (a mixture
  of apple, grape and
  pineapple is great)

Blend together the fruit juice, yogurt, banana, cinnamon, cloves and honey.

In a bowl, mix together the various fruits. Pour the blended mixture over them and stir until it's well-mixed. This is especially nice chilled before serving.

Variation:
Serve into individual bowls and top each one with a big dab of sour cream pre-mixed with honey.

Yield: *4-6 servings*

Serve the soups with toast, rolls or crackers.

Veggie Melt

1 ½ lbs. fresh broccoli
1 ½ Tbsp. olive or
   safflower oil
2 Tbsp. butter
1 small onion, thinly sliced
1 clove garlic
1 tsp. mixed Italian
   seasonings
2 oz. sliced black olives
¾ c. grated sharp cheddar
   cheese
1 vegetable bouillon cube
3 Tbsp. whole wheat pastry
   flour

Yield: 3-4 servings

Steam the broccoli until tender.

In a saucepan, heat the oil and add the onion and garlic. Saute over medium-low heat until golden and then add the butter. When melted, add the flour and stir until well-mixed with no lumps.

Dissolve the bouillon in 1¼ cups of boiling water and add this to the saucepan. Let the mixture continue to cook over medium-low heat until it thickens. Then add the cheese, seasonings, and olives, stirring until the cheese melts completely.

Place the broccoli in a casserole dish and pour the mixture over it.

This goes well with garlic bread or rolls.

Spiced Cream of Wheat

The people of South India eat this wholesome and nutritious dish—known as "Uppuma" (oo-poo-mah)—any time they want a quick, light meal and even for breakfast.

1 c. "Wheat Hearts"
   (whole wheat style
   cream of wheat)
2 c. water
1 carrot, chopped small
½ c. of cauliflower,
   chopped into small
   flowerettes
½ small onion, chopped
handful of cashews
¼ c. frozen peas
¼ tsp. turmeric
1 tsp. salt
3 Tbsp. oil
1 thin slice of ginger
½ tsp. black mustard
   seeds (Indian grocers)

First, roast the cream of wheat in a frying pan on a low heat until you begin to smell the aroma of the wheat and it is lightly roasted (about 5-10 minutes). Stir often so it does not burn.

In a saucepan, heat the oil and when hot, drop in the mustard seeds. They will sizzle and then pop, but take care not to let them burn. Heat the oil just enough, and then reduce the flame so that the seeds pop and don't start flying out of the pot. Then add the onion and let it saute until soft. Add the ginger and then the vegetables and cook until soft. Then add the turmeric, salt and cashews.

Add the water and let the mixture come to a vigorous boil. When it does, slowly begin to pour in the cream of wheat, slightly reducing the heat and constantly stirring to be sure the cream of wheat doesn't become lumpy and doesn't stick to the bottom of the pan. The cream of wheat should cook within 5-7 minutes. Then turn off the heat, place a pat of butter on top of the uppuma and let it sit covered for about 5-10 minutes. This allows it to finish cooking. The consistency is much thicker than the cream of wheat cereal consistency you are probably used to. The grains should be cooked to a thick, almost firm consistency.

Serve hot with yogurt as a side dish.

Yield: 2-3 servings

SANDWICHES & SPREADS

Tofu Salad Sandwich/Spread

8 oz. of tofu
2 Tbsp. safflower or soy
   mayonnaise
1 tsp. ketchup
1 clove garlic
1 Tbsp. chopped onion
1 tsp. honey (if desired)
¼ tsp. pepper
¼ tsp. cumin powder
½ tsp. basil
½ tsp. oregano
½ tsp. salt or use 1 tsp. of
   any vegetable salt like
   Vegit, Spike, Herbamare,
   etc.
½ tsp. tamari

Blend the ingredients together in a food processor or you can blend them in a bowl using a fork and some elbow grease! A coarser blend is nice for a sandwich, and a smooth blend makes a lovely dip or a spread for crackers, toast.

Fun to serve on whole-grain bread topped with chopped black olives or on a bun with raw onion rings.

Yield: 4 servings

Quick-Style "Pizza"

4 whole wheat English
muffins or 4 whole-
wheat pita breads
Homemade (or
commercial) pizza or
spaghetti sauce
1 cup of grated mozzarella
or soyarella cheese
basil and/or oregano

Split the muffins in half (if using pita bread, slice it open into two halves) and lightly toast.

Spread a good helping of sauce on the bread, sprinkle on the basil and/or oregano and top with cheese. Broil and serve bubbly hot.

Variations:

Add your own pizza toppings of onions (can be sauteed beforehand and then added on top), sliced or chopped olives, green pepper etc.

Create a Mexican flair by adding some ground cumin and/or chili powder to the sauce.

Rainbow Pasta Salad

3 c. rainbow-colored
whole-wheat or sesame
macaroni
¾ c. safflower or soy
mayonnaise
2 Tbsp. apple-cider vinegar
¾ c. diced celery
½ an onion, sliced thinly
¼ c. black olives sliced
½ tsp. oregano
½ tsp. basil
1 tsp. garlic salt
1 tsp. vegetable salt
¼ tsp. black pepper

Yield: 3-4 servings

Cook the macaroni until tender but not too soft (or it will break up in this type of salad). Drain, rinse in cold water and drain again.

In a mixing bowl, place all the rest of the ingredients and mix together well. Then add the macaroni and mix until it is well-coated. Add a few sprigs of parsley or fresh cilantro as a garnish.

Premala's Angel Cream

Guaranteed to send you to heaven! This is a wonderful evening fruit dish or a dessert served any time.

11 oz. mandarin oranges
(canned), drained
15 oz. can of crushed or
chunk-style pineapple,
drained
1 c. grated coconut
½ pint of sour cream
1 tin of canned mango
slices, chopped
(optional — can be
found at Indian grocers)

Mix all the ingredients in a large serving dish and cover the top with the coconut. Best to chill several hours before serving.

Appendix

Notes and References

PART 1

1. Ornish, D. M., Scherwitz, L. W., Doody, R. S., et al. "Effects of Stress Management Training and Dietary Changes in Treating Ischemic Heart Disease," Journal of the American Medical Association. Vol. 249, p. 5459, 1983

2. Ornish, D. M., Gotto, A. M., Miller, R. R., et al. "Effects of a Vegetarian Diet and Selective Yoga Techniques in the Treatment of Coronary Heart Disease," Clinical Research, Vol. 27, p. 720A, 1979

3. Scharffenberg, John A. *Problems with Meat as Human Food*, Woodbridge Press, Santa Barbara, 1979

4. Ornish, Dean, M. D. *Stress, Diet and Your Heart*, New American Library. New York, 1982

5. Lappe, Frances Moore. *Diet for a Small Planet*, Ballantine Books. New York, 1975

PART 2

1. For further information on Hatha Yoga techniques, instructions and benefits, please consult *Integral Yoga Hatha*, by Sri Swami Satchidananda; Holt, Reinhart and Winston. New York, 1970

2. Ibid

3. Ibid

4. Ibid

Resources

ORGANIZATIONS

There are numerous organizations now that exist solely to propagate vegetarianism. The International Vegetarian Union is the largest and oldest organization linking the majority of societies and associations around the world. The IVU sponsors annual congresses that feature speakers and workshops on the subjects of vegetarianism and health.

The North American Vegetarian Society (NAVS), in upstate New York, is an affiliate of the IVU which has nearly 60 local organizations and information centers from Maine to Hawaii and also in Canada. It organizes the annual World Vegetarian Congresses and World Vegetarian Day (October 1) celebrations.

NAVS works full-time to further the cause of vegetarianism on all levels including fostering a basic attitude of "reverence for life" and respect for the environment. They organize meetings, conferences and help research, publish and distribute literature about vegetarianism.

A great deal of information about vegetarianism is available by mail or by joining one of the societies and attending meetings.

Partial Listing of NAVS Organizations
(Please contact either the IVU or the NAVS for complete listings and further information about activities.):

International Vegetarian Union
10 King's Drive
Marple
Stockport
Cheshire, SK6 6NQ
England

International Vegetarian Union
North American Regional Office
P.O. Box 9710
Washington, D.C. 20016

The North American Vegetarian Society
P.O. Box 72
Dolgeville, NY 13329

The American Vegan Society
501 Old Harding Highway
Malaga, NJ 08328

Friends Vegetarian Society of North America
P.O. Box 53168
Washington, D.C. 20009

Cultural Media Services, Inc.
P.O. Box 1598
Soquel, CA 95073
(produces radio programs and cassettes on vegetarianism)

Baltimore Vegetarians
Jewish Vegetarians of North America
P.O. Box 1463
Baltimore, MD 21203

The Toronto Vegetarian Society
28 Walker Avenue
Toronto, Ontario M4V 1G2
Canada

Afro-American Vegetarian Society
P.O. Box 46
Colonial Park Station
New York, NY 10039

Vegetarian Information Service
P.O. Box 70123
Washington, D.C. 20088

Vegetarian Society, Inc.
P.O. Box 5688
Santa Monica, CA 90405

Vegetarian Gourmet Society
P.O. Box 8060
Hollywood, FL 33084

Vegetarian Society of Colorado
765 South Pennsylvania
Denver, CO 80209

Vegetarian Society of D.C.
P.O. Box 4921
Washington, D.C. 20008

Vegetarian Dietitians and Nutrition Educators
1225 Lenox Avenue
Miami Beach, FL 33139

Vancouver Island Vegetarian Assoc.
c/o Pat Bastone
9675 Fifth Street
Sidney, BC V8L 2W9
Canada
(an active group, but not a NAVS affiliate)

PUBLICATIONS

Journals (Also contact local groups for available newsletters)

Vegetarian Voice is published four times a year by the North American Vegetarian Society. You can write to them for subscription information.

The Friendly Vegetarian is published quarterly by the Friends Vegetarian Society of North America.

Vegetarian Times
141 South Oak Park Avenue
P.O. Box 570
Oak Park, IL 60303

East-West Journal
233 Harvard Street
Brookline, MA 02146

Yoga Journal
P.O. Box 15203
Santa Anna, CA 94704

New Age Journal
342 Western Avenue
Brighton, MA 02135

BOOKS

Diet and Nutrition

Ballentine, Rudolph. 1982. *Diet and Nutrition*. Honesdale, PA: Himalayan International Institute.

Lappe, Frances More. 1982. *Diet for a Small Planet: 10th Anniversary Edition*. New York, NY: Ballantine Books.

Ornish, Dean, M.D. 1982. *Stress, Diet and Your Heart*. New York, NY: New American Library.

Phillips, David A. 1979. *Guidebook to Nutritional Factors in Food*. Santa Barbara, CA: Woodbridge Press.

Cookbooks

Acciardo, Marcia. 1977. *Light Eating for Survival*. Wethersfield, CT: Omango D'Press.

Ballentine, Martha. 1976. *Himalayan Mountain Cookery*. Honesdale, PA: Himalayan International Institute.

Cherniske, Stephen. 1980. *Tofu, Everybody's Guide*. East Woodstock, CT: Mother's Inn Center for Creative Living.

Hagler, Louise. 1975. *The Farm Vegetarian Cookbook*. Summertown, TN: Book Publishing Company.

--- 1982. *Tofu Cookery*. Summertown, TN: Book Publishing Company.

Hurd, Frank, and Hurd, Rosalie. 1968. *Ten Talents*. Collegedale, TN: College Press.

Katzen, Mollie. 1977. *The Moosewood Cookbook*. Berkeley, CA: Ten Speed Press.

--- 1982. *The Enchanted Broccoli Forest*. Berkeley, CA: Ten Speed Press.

Kloss, Jethro. 1974. *The Back to Eden Cookbook*. Santa Barbara, CA: Lifeline Books.

Praver, Asha, and Gilchrist, Sheila. 1985. *The Ananda Cookbook*. Nevada City, CA: Ananda Publications.

Pride, Coleen. 1984. *Tempeh Cookery*. Summertown, TN: Book Publishing Company

Robertson, Laurel; Flinders, Carol; and Godfrey, Bronwen. 1976. *Laurel's Kitchen*. Petaluma, CA: Nilgiri Press.

Shurtleff, William, and Aoyagi, Akiko. *The Book of Tofu*. 1975. New York, NY: Ballantine Books.

--- 1984. *Tofu and Soymilk Production: The Book of Tofu, Vol. II*. Lafayette, LA: Soyfoods Center.

Zurbel, Victor, and Zurbel, Runa. 1978. *The Vegetarian Family*. Englewood Cliffs, NJ: Prentice-Hall, Inc.

Special Cuisines

Annechild, Annette. 1980. *Getting into Your Wok*. New York, NY: Wallaby Books. (Not solely vegetarian, but still a good reference book for wok cooking)

Jaffrey, Madhur. 1981. *Madhur Jaffrey's World of the East: Vegetarian Cooking*. New York, NY: Alfred A. Knopf.

Lo, Kenneth H.C. 1974. *Chinese Vegetarian Cooking*. New York, NY: antheon Books.

Romagnolis, Margaret, and Romagnolis, G. Franco. 1976. *The Romagalis' Meatless (Italian) Cookbook*. Boston, MA: Little, Brown and Company.

Santa Maria, Jack. 1977. *Indian Vegetarian Cookery*. New York, NY: Samuel Weiser, Inc.

Sacharoff, Shanta Nimbark. 1972. *Flavors of India*. San Francisco, CA: 101 Productions.

About Children

Gross, Joy, and Freifield, Karen. 1983. *The Vegetarian Child*. Secaucus, NJ: Lyle Stuart.

Shandler, Michael, and Shandler, Nina. 1981. *The Complete Guide and Cookbook for Raising Your Child as a Vegetarian*. New York, NY: Schocken Books.

Zurbel, Victor, and Zurbel, Runa. 1984. *The Natural Lunchbox*. New York, NY: Holt, Rinehart and Winston.

For Children

Hurwitz, Johanna. 1978. *Much Ado About Aldo*. New York, NY: William Morrow.

Lambert, Joyce. 1962. *How To Be Kind*. Fredericton, New Brunswick, Canada: New Brunswick Press.

Yoga

Integral Yoga Publications. 1979. *Integral Yoga Hatha* Booklet and Cassette Tape (available in Beginners I, Beginners II and a 30-minute version). Pomfret Center, CT: Integral Yoga Publications.

Satchidananda, Sri Swami. 1970. *Integral Yoga Hatha*. New York, NY: Holt, Rinehart and Winston.

Glossary

Glossary of Sanskrit Words

ahimsa — non-injury; first of the "ten commandments" of *Raja Yoga*

ashram — a spiritual community where seekers practice and study under the guidance of a spiritual master

ayurveda — (lit. scripture of life) one of the Indian systems of medicine

Bhagavad Gita — Hindu scripture in which Lord Krishna instructs his disciple Arjuna in the various aspects of Yoga

bhoga — enjoyment; *bhogi* — one who enjoys

guna — one of the qualities of nature: *sattva, rajas* and *tamas* or balance, activity and inertia

guru — (lit. remover of darkness) spiritual guide, teacher

Hatha Yoga — the physical aspect of Yoga practice, including postures, breathing techniques, seals, locks and cleansing practices

kapha — (in *ayurveda*) mucus-producing

karma — action and reaction

karuna — mercy, compassion

kriya — action, practice; (*Hatha Yoga*) cleansing practice

maha vratam — (lit. great vows) refers to the *yamas* or abstinences of Yoga: non-violence, truthfulness, non-stealing, continence and non-greed

pitta—(in *ayurveda*) bile-producing

prana—the vital energy

pranayama—the practice of controlling the vital force, usually through control of the breath

pratyahara—sense control; withdrawal of the senses from their objects

Raja Yoga—the "Royal Yoga;" the system of concentration and meditation based on ethical discipline

rajas—activity, restlessness (one of the three *gunas* or qualities of nature)

roga—disease; *rogi* — a diseased person

sattva—purity; balanced state (one of the three *gunas* or qualities of nature)

swami—renunciate; monk initiated into the Holy Order of Sannyas

tamas—inertia, dullness (one of the three *gunas* or qualities of nature)

vata—(in *ayurveda*) wind-producing

Yoga—(lit. union) union of the individual with the Absolute; any course that makes for such union; unruffled state of mind under all conditions

Reverend Sri Swami Satchidananda

"Naturally, I'm a vegetarian..."

Sri Swami Satchidananda is one of the most revered living Yoga Masters of our time. A much-loved teacher, well known in today's world for his combination of spiritual wisdom and practical insight, he has given his life to the service of humanity, demonstrating by his own example the means of finding abiding peace within one's life and within one's self.

Sri Swamiji does not belong to any one faith, group or country. Dedicated to the principle that "Truth is One, Paths are Many," he goes wherever he is asked to serve, bringing together people of all backgrounds and beliefs. Through his guidance and inspiration, people all over the globe have learned to respect all the different paths, realizing their common spirit and the universality of their goal. The LOTUS (Light Of Truth Universal Shrine) at Satchidananda Ashram—Yogaville, Virginia, is a place where all can come together to realize that one Truth behind all the names and forms.

Sri Swamiji has been a vegetarian since birth, and has been a firm believer in *ahimsa*—non-violence in thought, word and deed—all of his life. He is a living example of the goal of Yoga (living an easeful, peaceful, useful life) and of the radiant health, balanced mind, keen intellect, pliable will, compassionate heart, and realization of the ultimate Truth that is the birthright of us all.